MICHIGAN'S
CON-CON 11

MICHIGAN'S CON-CON 11

Women and State Constitution-making in 1961

Lynn Liberato

MICHIGAN STATE UNIVERSITY PRESS | *East Lansing*

Michigan State University Press
East Lansing, Michigan 48823-5245

Library of Congress Cataloging-in-Publication Data is available
ISBN 978-1-61186-553-0 (Paper)
ISBN 978-1-60917-797-3 (PDF)
ISBN 978-1-62895-560-6 (ePub)

Book design by Anastasia Wraight
Cover design by David Drummond

Visit Michigan State University Press at *www.msupress.org*

For
Vera Andrus
Ruth Butler
Anne Conklin
Katherine Cushman
Ann Donnelly
Daisy Elliott
Adelaide Hart
Lillian Hatcher
Dorothy Judd
Ella Koeze
Marjorie McGowan

And to my father—Ralph A. Liberato, Con-Con delegate from the 11th Senatorial District—who inspired this journey

Con-Con 11 (*left to right*): Ella Koeze, Daisy Elliott, Anne Conklin, Ann Donnelly, Lillian Hatcher, Marjorie McGowan, Adelaide Hart, Dorothy Judd, Ruth Butler, Vera Andrus and Katherine Cushman. (KATHERINE MOORE CUSHMAN CON-CON COLLECTION. COURTESY OF BETSY CUSHMAN.)

Contents

Preface

The Con-Con story I wanted to tell was my father's story. He was a delegate to the 1961–62 Michigan Constitutional Convention. We never discussed the convention, however, and he left no personal records upon which I could base a book. After his passing, I found his copy of the *Official Record* and a scrapbook full of newspaper clippings. I remembered the articles. Even as a child I couldn't help but notice the headlines blaring Con-Con *this* and Con-Con *that*. I grasped that Con-Con was important, but had no clue what it was other than the place where Dad spent the week doing whatever people who went to Con-Con did. And yet, my fascination with Con-Con never left me. For years I read and reread those articles, wondering why they resonated with me so strongly.

After retirement I perused the *Official Record* from time to time and began to grasp the enormity of Con-Con's significance. The 3,353-page verbatim transcript of the convention was intimidating. I found I could not read more than a few pages without feeling like I was back in law school. Still, I knew I wanted to write about the convention.

Writing about other male delegates seemed disloyal. If I couldn't tell my father's story, I didn't want to tell anyone's. Then I realized that there were only eleven women delegates. They also happened to be the first female delegates elected to a Michigan constitutional convention. Eleven female delegates and 133 male delegates. Now that could be a story! And I felt no disloyalty writing about the women. I also think my father would have approved. Shortly after I decided to write this book, my father appeared to me in a dream. I told him that I was going to need to interview him for my Con-Con book. He slowly nodded and said that he would help me. We agreed to meet the next day. Then I woke up.

Introduction

When Michigan's 5th Constitutional Convention (Con-Con)
convened on October 3, 1961, the 1908 constitution was
in dire need of revision and modernizing. In many ways,
the state was operating under a constitution that was
more than one hundred years old because the 1908 constitution was a
slight revision of the 1850 Constitution.[1] Significant technological and
social changes had occurred since 1908. When Michigan's last constitutional convention delegates met in 1907, Henry Ford was on the brink of
producing the Model T. By 1961, astronauts were being sent into outer
space. Michigan's population had increased 178.3 percent from 1910 to
1960. In 1910, more than half of the population lived in rural areas. By
1960, nearly three quarters of the population lived in urban areas, with
53 percent living in Wayne, Washtenaw, Oakland and Macomb counties.[2]
Michigan had transitioned from an agricultural state to an industrial
giant and a tourist and car manufacturing mecca.

Con-Con's 1961 delegates needed to make the state's highest law
flexible enough to last at least fifty years and workable for the present.

The constitution had a patchwork quality after having been amended sixty-nine times. New sections needed to be added. Irrelevant sections needed to be removed. Many sections needed to be restructured and rephrased. The constitution was too long and too detailed. By 1960, the Michigan Constitution had grown to 21,790 words.[3]

The calling of the 1961 Michigan Constitutional Convention was truly a citizen's victory. Many state employee groups such as the County Road Association of Michigan, Farm Bureau, Sherriff's Association and Michigan Townships Association had been opposed, and Michigan's two major political parties were divided on whether or not a convention should be called. The Con-Con victory was largely made possible by three nonpartisan citizens groups: the League of Women Voters of Michigan, Citizens for Michigan and the Michigan Junior Chamber of Commerce (Jaycees).[4]

Reapportionment of the state legislature and fiscal reform drove the call for a convention. The Michigan Senate was severely malapportioned. Although the 1908 constitution required that the Senate be apportioned on a population basis every ten years, the legislature stopped reapportioning itself after the 1920s. A 1952 constitutional amendment only made matters worse. In 1958, Oakland County held more than twelve times the number of persons of an outstate district, yet each district elected one senator.[5] The disparity gave rural areas disproportional influence in the legislature.

By 1959, Michigan was in the midst of a full-blown financial crisis. Although it was resolved fairly quickly, the crisis left Michiganders anxious for constitutional reforms. Some wondered whether a graduated income tax should be included in the new constitution and if earmarking should be continued. Five-sixths of the state sales tax revenue was constitutionally earmarked for schools and local government units, thereby significantly usurping legislative control over state funds. Causes of Michigan's financial mess were rooted in the constitutional structure, and many blamed the governor and legislature for failing to agree on a tax program. Distrust of and disappointment in the legislature was at an all-time high.

The executive branch needed streamlining. The state's 126 administrative agencies had become unmanageable. Many felt that extending the term of office for the governor and other state officials from two to four years would assist them in carrying out their duties.

Civil rights were a pressing concern. Unlike other states, Michigan's constitution did not include an equal protection clause. Increased fiscal and operating autonomy for local government units and authorization for intergovernmental agreements in metropolitan areas was sought.[6] The Michigan League of Women Voters advocated for county home rule. The 1908 constitution only provided for municipal home rule. These were but a few of the changes delegates hoped to see in the new constitution.

Momentum for a constitutional convention had been slowly building since 1926. The question of whether or not a convention should be called was automatically placed on the ballot every sixteen years, pursuant to Article XVII of the 1908 constitution. The referendum lost. The question next appeared on the ballot in 1942. By this time, interest in a convention had been growing for several years. In 1938, Governor Frank Murphy created the Commission on Reform and Modernization of Government to stimulate interest in constitutional reform. In 1941, Governor Murray D. Van Wagoner created a constitutional revision study commission by executive order to provide guidance on the question of whether or not a constitutional convention should be called. But the referendum still lost.

The next attempt to call a convention occurred in 1948 when the legislature submitted the question on its own initiative.[7] World War II was over and many people felt there was a better chance for success. The League of Women Voters supported the 1948 ballot proposal.[8] Although a majority of the people voting on the question favored calling a convention, the majority of the people voting in the election did not, and the proposal failed.[9] Although 855,451 votes were cast in favor of—and 799,198 votes were cast against—calling a Con-Con, the call was defeated due to the constitutional requirement of a majority of votes cast in the election.[10]

The league spent the next decade studying Michigan government and preparing for 1958 when the question would automatically appear on the ballot.[11] The league picked up an invaluable ally and a much-needed morale boost when the Jaycees put the Con-Con issue on their state program. Other supporting groups included the Michigan Education Association, the American Association of University Women, the

Michigan Municipal League and the Michigan Congress of Parents and Teachers. But the league launched the most intensive campaign. League members made some 800 speeches, circulated some 150,000 flyers and poll handouts, presented numerous skits and persuaded the media and other organizations to get on board. However, the proposal failed again for the same reasons it had failed in 1926, 1942 and 1948. It did not receive a majority of votes cast by electors, although a majority voting on the question clearly favored calling a convention.[12] The momentum to call another convention would continue to increase.

In late 1959, the Jaycees presented the league with a proposed amendment that would simplify the calling of a convention.[13] Instead of requiring a majority of electors to approve a Con-Con, the proposed amendment only required a majority of voters voting on the question. The amendment also altered the basis of representation by authorizing one convention delegate from each state House and Senate district. In November 1960, the Gateway Amendment appeared on the ballot as Proposal 3. It was approved 1,312,215 to 959,527.[14] A proposal to call a convention was placed on the April 3, 1961, ballot. The proposal passed, and a July 25th primary and a September 12th general election were held to elect Con-Con delegates. Pursuant to the legislative act, delegates were required to run on a partisan basis.[15] Voters elected 144 Con-Con delegates—one from each existing House and Senate district. Of the 144 delegates, 13 were African American and 11 were women. It was the first time women and African Americans were elected to help rewrite Michigan's highest law.

I.

Opening Day

Veteran's Auditorium
Lansing Civic Center
October 3, 1961

The inaugural session of Michigan's 5th Constitutional Convention (Con-Con) was about to begin. Inside the Lansing Civic Center, Convention and Visitor Council members greeted delegates as information booth girls stood by ready to help. Everyone wore badges. Flashbulbs popped like a fireworks finale. Michigan State University's radio and television stations broadcasted the event. High school students ushered delegates to their tables inside the Civic Center's Veteran's Auditorium. The main auditorium was being used for the opening day ceremonies. The specially remodeled smaller auditorium—which would officially be known as Constitution Hall would be where the actual convention took place. Inside the Veteran's Auditorium, a high school band played the spirited Notre Dame fight song.[1] Delegates and attendees didn't need the adrenaline boost. Energy levels inside the auditorium were already off the charts.

Daisy

After a frosty fall night, Con-Con's opening day would be sunny and warm. It was a good sign. Daisy Elliott believed in signs. When an astrologer told her to wait before purchasing an apartment building, she listened. She later bought the building at a lower price.[2] But mostly, Elliott believed in herself. The coal miner's daughter from West Virginia *knew* she was destined for greater things. After five unsuccessful runs for state representative, Elliott finally scored her first public office win when she was elected to Con-Con.[3] Fortunately for Elliott, more opportunities existed for women to break through entrenched power structures in conventions than in legislatures.[4] And by the early 1960s, state constitutional conventions were being held in greater numbers around the country. "Timing is everything," as they say, and Elliott and the other female delegates were able to seize the moment. Women didn't have that opportunity when the prior convention met in 1907. They didn't even have the right to vote, let alone help rewrite Michigan's highest law. But women had gained a great deal of civic and political experience since 1907 through business women's clubs and the League of Women Voters. Running for Con-Con delegate also didn't require the same type of party backing as legislative or Congressional races. But Elliott had the backing of her party, unlike some of the other female delegates.

As a Con-Con delegate, Elliott couldn't have found a better training ground for the legislature. She understood that political office could be used as a tool to fight discrimination. A successful realtor and business owner, Elliott was a Renaissance Black—one of many professional and educated Black citizens who purchased stately homes in Detroit's Arden Park and Boston-Edison districts during the 1950s and 1960s.[5] Elliott often held gatherings at her "beautiful" and "spacious" Arden Park home to facilitate the many civic, social, political and religious groups and organizations in which she was involved.[6] By 1958, she was considered a prominent civic, social and political worker in Detroit and a church leader in the community.[7] Like the other twelve Black delegates, Elliott was committed to succeed where the legislature had failed in enacting important civil rights laws. It would be the first time African Americans and women would help rewrite Michigan's highest law. Never in her wildest dreams could Elliott have imagined that nearly sixty years later a state office building in downtown Lansing would be renamed for her.[8]

Vera

As crowds of people headed toward the Civic Center's main auditorium, Vera Andrus headed for the smaller auditorium in the Center's south wing. Constitution Hall was where the real action would take place the next day. Final touches were still being made to the remodeled auditorium to accommodate Con-Con's 144 delegates, the press and visitors. A painter was covering up patches in the corridor as Andrus strolled by.[9] Inside, workmen were hanging drapes behind the speaker's rostrum. The retired college administrator and instructor couldn't resist checking out her new classroom. She was ready. After teaching government classes for thirty-seven years and working for changes in local and state government, the League of Women Voters leader was embracing this historic once-in-a-lifetime opportunity. Andrus wanted a new section in the constitution that would support and govern community and junior colleges. No one understood better than she how community colleges could fill the widening gap in higher education and skills training.

A consummate educator, campaign photos showed the matronly looking Andrus standing at the front of a classroom, pointer in hand. The sixty-five-year-old Andrus had never run for public office before, but what she lacked in funds, political experience and support, she made up for in effort and ingenuity. She knocked on more doors than her male opponents and mobilized friends and former students into a highly effective grassroots campaign. Her efforts paid off. She was the top vote getter in her district. After winning the July 25, 1961, primary election, she took an ad out in the local paper to thank her friends and students for their support. Andrus's students had urged her to run for Con-Con. For Andrus, it was always about the students. The young people. She was a hard taskmaster who asked much, but also gave much, and her students had loved her for it. She would do everything in her power to help write a new constitution—a better constitution—for young people and their descendants.

Anne

Welcome banners waved at Anne Conklin from utility poles as city, state and convention flags flapped in the warm autumn breeze.[10] Scores of red, white and blue "Welcome Con-Con" signs depicting the capital and downtown Lansing skyline greeted her from the windows of local businesses. It had been fifty-four years since Michigan's capital had hosted a constitutional convention, and Lansing had pulled out all the stops to make delegates feel welcomed. The prior evening's reception dinner had been a lavish affair, and the civic reception at the Jack Tar Hotel after the inaugural session would be the same. The reception would give delegates an opportunity to meet newspaper, radio and television reporters who would be covering the convention. City and state officials, along with members from the governor's Preparatory Commission, would also be present.

Despite having a passion for politics, the thirty-six-year-old Conklin had never considered running for office. The Livonia housewife and mother of three had been content to be a party worker. Conklin didn't give politics much thought until she got involved in a school issue campaign. She later became president of the Livonia Republican Women's Club, a member of the Republican State Central Committee and an alternate delegate to the 1956 Republican National Convention. She also served as a secretary of the Livonia Community Council and as a member of the Board of Education Advisory Committee. From 1958 through 1960, Conklin was a paid executive GOP County secretary. During that time, she worked as a secretary in U.S. Representative Alvin Bentley's unsuccessful senatorial campaign. It didn't take party members long to notice the petite brunette with the bubbling personality. When a group of Livonia Republicans asked her to run for Con-Con, Conklin was flabbergasted and scared. She had seven opponents. Like Con-Con's other ten women, Conklin campaigned hard and went door-to-door to pass out literature. Although the high school graduate was intimidated to debate a well-educated teacher, she did well enough to obtain the support of the American Association of University Women. Conklin then won her Con-Con seat in a district that hadn't elected a Republican since 1956. As fate would have it, Bentley was also elected as a delegate.

Katherine

The first thing Katherine Cushman noticed as she entered Veteran's Auditorium was the bright-green floor covering and the huge American flag backdrop. As she followed a high school student to her seat, Cushman could see that all of the delegate tables were adorned with brightly colored floral bouquets. It was hard not to be moved. Her Con-Con journey had started years before. As a League of Women Voters leader, Cushman had been very active in league efforts to get a constitutional convention called. Cushman had been president of the Detroit League of Women Voters from 1943 to 1949 and became a member of the Dearborn chapter in 1951. The Dearborn League began campaigning for a convention in 1955. Members stood outside the Ford Rouge plant for days in 90-degree heat getting signatures and educating people on the need for a constitutional convention. Cushman gave talks, wrote letters and organized poll workers.

League efforts to get a Con-Con called started even earlier. In 1948, the league supported a ballot proposal that asked Michigan voters to decide whether or not a constitutional convention should be called. Although a majority of the people voting on the question favored calling a convention, the majority of the people voting in the election did not, and the proposal failed. The league then spent the next decade studying Michigan government and preparing for 1958, when the Con-Con question would automatically appear on the ballot.[11] The league picked up an invaluable ally when the Michigan Jaycees put the constitutional convention issue on their state program. Other organizations, like the Michigan Education Association and Parent Teacher Association, also began to slowly offer support, but the league launched the most intensive campaign. League members made approximately 800 speeches, circulated some 150,000 flyers and poll handouts, presented numerous skits and persuaded the media and other organizations to get on board. The proposal failed, however, for the same reason it had failed in 1948. The tide began to turn in late 1959, when the Jaycees presented the league with a proposed amendment that would simplify the way a constitutional convention would be called. Instead of requiring a majority of electors to approve a Con-Con, the proposed amendment only required the approval of a majority of voters voting on the question. In November 1960, the amendment appeared on the ballot as Proposal 3.

The petition drive to put the amendment on the ballot almost failed despite the league's almost Herculean efforts to obtain signatures. League members were noted for their tenacity, and some individual members obtained 1,000 to 1,200 signatures. Despite their efforts, the league needed help to meet the deadline.[12] The newly formed nonpartisan group Citizens for Michigan came to the rescue. So did Cushman's husband, Ed. American Motors Corporation (AMC) vice president Edward Cushman cofounded Citizens for Michigan with his boss, AMC president George Romney, in December 1959. The two men shared Cushman's passion for good government. Thus, when it became apparent that the league would not meet the deadline for petition signatures, Ed asked Michigan teachers to each get a petition with thirty signatures. Citizens for Michigan distributed petitions to teachers and sent thousands of petitions to the Michigan Education Association summer camp for teachers at St. Mary's Lake. Within six weeks, Citizens for Michigan received "a tremendous number of signatures."[13] Citizens for Michigan also provided much-needed funding that the league lacked. The amendment passed.

Although Cushman ran as a Democrat, her Con-Con candidacy was not supported by organized labor or the Democratic party. No doubt they were concerned about her close ties to Romney, who ran for Con-Con as a Republican. The Romneys and Cushmans were also good friends. But Cushman and Romney were independents at heart, required by law to run on a partisan basis. Still, many people wondered if Cushman would be influenced by her husband's boss. One newspaper article even stated that AMC would have a voice on both sides. It wouldn't take long, however, for everyone to realize that Cushman had a mind of her own.

Adelaide

Adelaide Hart made a point to greet Detroit delegate Coleman Young as she entered the delegate seating area. Hart was angry that the Democratic party had failed to invite Young to its first meeting with the delegates. Some people still viewed Young as a communist because he had been called in front of the House Un-American Activities Committee in 1952 for being a suspected Communist Party member.[14] Although he always denied the allegation and was never proven to be a communist, some Democrats still shunned him. Hart, a former vice chairman of the Democratic State Central Committee, was not going to tolerate any in-fighting. As the Democratic caucus chair at Con-Con, Hart needed to keep the Dems organized, effective and unified. Democratic delegates were outnumbered by Republicans ninety-nine to forty-five. At the meeting that Young had not been invited to, Hart quickly made, seconded and passed the first motion: "that every Democrat that was elected be welcomed as long as they act like Democrats."[15] Hart didn't allow a vote on her motion. Afterwards, she took Young around and introduced him to the other delegates.[16] Years later, Hart would recall that Young was one of the most dedicated and hard-working Democrats at the convention. (Young later went on to become Detroit's first Black and longest-serving mayor.)

Hart was a legend among Democrats. The Detroit school teacher was known as the conscience of the party organization.[17] Hart never missed a campaign or planning meeting, even when they were held on school days or in Lansing. Sometimes while driving home from Lansing, she would pull over beside the road to nap if she got too sleepy. More than once she would be awakened by a state trooper rapping on her window to make sure she was all right. Hart was one of the New Democrats credited with revitalizing the Democratic party in Michigan. G. Mennen "Soapy" Williams's twelve-year gubernatorial reign marked the Golden Age of the Democratic party in Michigan. Williams respected and trusted Hart. Endearing stories of how the diminutive Hart would shake her finger in the face of the towering Williams and tell him what's what circulated among Democrats for years. Even Republicans added to the Hart lore. After Hart was accidentally knocked backwards down a flight of stairs during a 17th congressional district meeting skirmish, Republicans used the incident as a radio skit and ad called "Blood on the Pavement."[18] Although Hart was not hurt, she had taken one for the team, which further endeared her to Democrats. Hart was also credited with bringing more women into the Democratic party. She wanted women to understand the issues and be part of the decision-making process. She dreamed of a federation of Democratic women.

Hart knew she would have her work cut out for her. She would also set an example. Although some Democrats were galled at being called the minority party after controlling the governor's office since 1949, Hart was not one of them. She reminded Dems that they needed to be gracious in defeat. They needed to be gracious and effective. Hart would have to utilize her many talents and powers of persuasion with some of the younger, second-generation Democrats, as well as with independents.[19] Hart would also keep her eyes on Romney. Romney was acting a lot like a gubernatorial candidate and the press was treating him like one.

Ella

While Hart watched Romney, GOP National Committeewoman Ella Koeze watched everyone. Koeze loved politics. The Grand Rapids native felt she had invaded men's territory by running for Con-Con. Koeze came from a heavily Dutch-populated area where women were expected to stay home. But Con-Con was the political event of a lifetime, and Koeze wanted a front row seat. Koeze was pleased that delegates unanimously elected Stephen Nisbet as convention president. The gentlemanly Nisbet was well liked and respected by both parties. He may have been a compromise candidate, but he would turn out to be the right choice. As a mother of five grown children, Koeze knew a lot about compromise and tackling unpleasant jobs. She was not a squeamish woman. When her sons were young, she skinned muskrats and cleaned pheasants that they hunted and trapped on the family estate. She also tolerated her husband's collection of pigeons, peacocks, oriental pheasants, swans, ducks and quail even though she detested them all. Her ability to compromise and roll with the punches made her an effective politician. She steadily rose through the ranks from 1940 when she became a precinct worker until 1960 when she was elected to the Republican National Committee.

Lillian

Like Elliott, Lillian Hatcher also ran for Con-Con on a platform of civil rights. Hatcher and Elliott were friends. Elliott had recently cohosted a bridal shower for Hatcher's youngest daughter and attended the wedding.[20] Now they both were making history together. Both were Prince Hall Masons and members of the 13th Congressional District Democratic Committee.[21] They shared memberships in the Current Topic Study Club, the Women's International League for Peace and Freedom, the Young Women's Christian Association (YWCA), the Detroit Urban League, the Detroit Chapter of the National Junior League and the National Council of Negro Women.[22] Like the other Black Con-Con delegates, they were also very active in the Democratic party and the Detroit branch of the National Association for the Advancement of Colored People (NAACP).

Both women had also done defense factory work during World War II, and both had experienced discrimination. As it had for many women, World War II changed Hatcher's life. She was able to earn considerably more in the defense industry. She also learned about unionism and how it could fight racial and gender discrimination. But even before Hatcher rose from factory worker to become the first Black female international representative for the United Auto Workers (UAW) assigned to the Women's Bureau in 1944, she gained organizing and leadership experience attending Double Victory Club meetings.[23] The Double V campaign became a rallying cry for Black people to obtain victory over fascism abroad and victory over racism at home. The Double V clubs—which often met at the local YWCA or nearby churches—motivated Hatcher to become more involved in the union. The clubs fought discrimination in restaurants and other public places. Double V members also performed outreach in the neighborhoods. Hatcher's husband also encouraged her unionism.

By 1946, Hatcher was assigned as a staffer in the UAW's Fair Employment Practices Department.[24] The name Lillian Hatcher generated admiration and respect from area Blacks and union workers. The beloved Hatcher had been appointed to important civil rights committees and worked tirelessly to fight gender and racial discrimination. Hatcher's years in the Women's Bureau taught her that sex- and race-based discriminations were just two sides of the same coin. Indeed, some women complained that they experienced more discrimination as a woman than as an African American.

The youthful-looking Hatcher was friends with many of the other Black Con-Con delegates. Morris Hood Sr. was one of the organizers of the first union Hatcher joined, UAW Local 742.[25] Morris's two sons, Morris Jr. and Raymond, endearingly called Hatcher "Mom" for being a loving and guiding presence in their lives.[26] Hatcher guided and became a humble role model for many others. Hatcher also worked with the Reverend Malcom Dade when the two civil rights leaders were appointed to the mayor's Citizens' Advisory Committee on Police Procedures in 1958 to address police brutality.[27] They also became members of the Commission on Community Relations that year.[28] Now they were both Con-Con delegates, and Reverend Dade was giving the first invocation of the convention. Hatcher couldn't have been prouder.

Dorothy

Dorothy Judd was happy to see some familiar faces sitting in the delegates' section. Judd, Andrus and Cushman were acquainted with one another through their League of Women Voters work. Now the three league leaders were staying at the Capitol Park Motor Hotel so that they could breakfast together and work on league interests like education, election laws, local and state government, taxation, civil service, civil rights and intergovernmental relations.[29] The new 147-room annex to the former Porter Hotel and Apartments had just opened several months earlier and was within walking distance of Constitution Hall.[30] Judd was also good friends with, and a former student of, University of Michigan political science professor James Pollock. The two had served on the Michigan State Civil Service Study Commission in 1935, and Judd looked forward to working with him again in Con-Con. Judd was also good friends with Michigan State University president John Hannah, who would become one of Con-Con's leaders.[31]

The elegant and erudite Judd had been a suffragist sympathizer when she was a student at Vassar College. As a Vassar student, Judd met such famous people as Eleanor Roosevelt and naturalist John Burroughs. Vassar was within bicycling distance of their homes, and both icons were in the habit of welcoming visiting Vassar girls. Judd remembered Roosevelt as a charming and welcoming person who shared many stories of her life in the White House. Judd always remembered her acquaintance with Roosevelt as one of the big pluses of attending Vassar. When suffragist leaders organized the League of Women Voters in Grand Rapids, Judd was one of the first to join.[32] She became the youngest League of Women Voters of Michigan president in 1927.

Ann

Uber-lawyer Ann Donnelly couldn't resist the opportunity to help revise the constitution's judicial article. The State Bar of Michigan had just held its annual meeting, and attorneys across the state had lots to say about how the judicial article should be improved. One of the hottest topics concerned the abolishment of the justice of the peace system. Donnelly intended to offer a delegate proposal to eliminate it. Of the fifty-seven lawyers elected to Con-Con, Donnelly was among the most respected.[33] She had graduated law school with high honors and may have created history when she set up practice with two other female attorneys in 1956. Female attorneys in Detroit at that time were estimated at less than twenty-five. Donnelly's firm may have been the first female law firm in Detroit or Michigan. At least that was the buzz among local attorneys.[34]

As a member of the State Bar Committee on Judicial Selection and Tenure and a member of the Detroit Bar Association and the Women Lawyers of Michigan, Donnelly was invested in the future of Michigan's legal system and profession.[35]

Marjorie

Thirty-one-year-old Detroit attorney Marjorie McGowan had an aha moment as she listened to Reverend Dade give the invocation and watched Black delegate Sidney Barthwell escort president-elect Nisbet to the podium. The visual of Barthwell, Michigan State University president Hannah and University of Michigan professor James Pollock walking to the podium with Nisbet was powerful. *This is how racial prejudices will change,* she thought. *Not by marches or boycotts, but by recognizing the value of African Americans like Barthwell and Reverand Dade.*

By all indications, McGowan was a rising civil rights leader. She had been a member of the Detroit branch of the NAACP at least since 1953, when she was elected secretary.[36] In 1960, Michigan's African American newspaper, the *Michigan Chronicle*, reported that McGowan was "creating a blaze within the civil rights division."[37] She was assigned to the newly created civil rights division in the Wayne County Prosecuting Attorney's office. She arranged for two white police officers to appear in a line-up based on a Black citizen's complaint, which was believed to have been the first such police line-up in the department's history.[38] McGowan was often written about in the *Michigan Chronicle*. The newspaper had been following her career since 1952, when McGowan graduated from law school.[39] Her personal and professional ascent began in 1958, when she was appointed as Wayne County's first Black female assistant prosecuting attorney. In 1960, she became the first Black woman to be selected as one of Detroit's ten outstanding working women. The soft-spoken, quiet-mannered McGowan earned a reputation as a "hard-hitting" prosecutor who won most of her cases.[40] Known for her "penetrating cross-examination," McGowan became the first female assistant prosecutor in the early morning sessions of Recorder's Court and earned the respect of judges, attorneys, detectives, policemen and fellow assistant prosecutors.[41] Detroit's Black population and the Democratic party expected great things from McGowan at Con-Con.

Ruth

Upper Peninsula delegate Ruth Butler couldn't sleep. She lay in bed at her son Gib's house replaying the last few days over in her mind. She was still up in the clouds and could scarcely believe such a wonderful experience was happening to her. Several nights earlier she had attended a small private dinner hosted by MSU president Hannah. Hannah had pulled out all the stops and reserved a private dining room at MSU's Kellogg Center for the small party. Butler had been impressed by the plush décor and service. That day Hannah and his wife had taken Butler under their wing at the Jack Tar Hotel reception. She knew she'd never remember half the people they introduced her to, but they would remember her because she was with the Hannahs. She was touched that they were looking out for the seventy-year-old grandmother and widow. They would become lifelong friends.

Butler had no illusions about the hard work ahead. She welcomed it. Meeting lots of new people would be healing. It would also be fun. Butler was a people person whose interest in politics was influenced by her charismatic politician father.[42] Unlike most of the delegates who rented rooms at local hotels, Butler rented an apartment in a private residence at 606 Cherry Street. Her landlady was president of the Lansing chapter of the Business and Professional Women's Club. A longtime member of the Houghton-Hancock chapter, Butler knew her Lansing club sisters would not let her get lonesome. She looked forward to moving in soon. But that night, she was at Gib's. Gib was a design engineer who lived and worked nearby. It warmed her heart that her only son was there to watch her take the oath of office. Gib had been so moved that he penned a tribute to his mother which he gave Butler later that evening. He compared delegates to the Founding Fathers. Butler may not have been a Founding Mother, but she would always share the distinction of being one of the first female delegates at a Michigan constitutional convention. Gib wanted Butler to know how proud he was of her and that he was confident she would serve all the people with her whole mind, body and soul. She was an old war horse, he said, who still had lots of fight and stamina and who could still subdue those much younger. He also knew that his mother would not be swayed by glamourous personalities or dignitaries. Just that morning an Iron Mountain lobbyist had treated her and the other U.P. delegates to breakfast. Butler was not impressed when the lobbyist tried to tell them what they should do. "Of course, none of us did it," she later wrote in a family letter.[43] Butler liked to sign her family letters "Ruthie with the Truthie." The other delegates would soon find out how appropriate that moniker was.

II

October 1961

D elegates gathered in Constitution Hall for Con-Con's second session. Con-Con's second day was not unlike the first day of school. Delegates tried out their new pedestal chairs, looked around to see who was seated near them, "winced at the array of literature that needed to be read, and fumbled in self-conscious attempts to get recognized from the chair."[1] All of the women were smartly dressed. For attorneys Ann Donnelly and Marjorie McGowan, it was just another day at the office. For Daisy Elliott, it was another chance to dress to impress. Years later when she was a state representative, Elliott would become known as "the fashion plate of the House."[2]

The room held a feeling of excitement. On one side of the auditorium the press box was crammed with reporters. On the other side was the visitor's gallery. There were also big windows along the back wall so that overflow crowds could peer into the auditorium. Working in a fishbowl would take some getting used to for delegates like Anne Conklin who had lived private lives before Con-Con. Desks were arranged in a semicircle, United Nations style, with delegates seated alphabetically to encourage interaction between the two parties. Dorothy Judd found the Herman Miller–style chairs comfortable. Judd was fascinated by the electronic buttons on each desk that displayed the names and votes of each delegate on a big board in red and white lights. She was glad that the men who installed the voting machines would be available after the session to answer questions. Ella Koeze found the desks much too small for all of the reading material that was sure to increase and would have preferred more elbow room. She decided that she would have an extra shelf built under her desk. Adelaide Hart took note of the microphones that were installed throughout to allow delegates to speak from the floor. It was important that Democrats, as the minority party, make a record of what they tried to accomplish at the convention. The rest of the women, like the rest of the delegates, were just trying to take it all in.

Republicans J. Edward Hutchinson and George Romney and Democrat Tom Downs were unanimously elected as the three convention vice presidents. Elliott was pleased that Downs was one of the convention leaders. Elliott and Reverend Malcolm Dade had run a successful Con-Con campaign with the American Federation of Labor and Congress of Industrial Organizations (AFL-CIO) attorney. The three Detroiters reflected Wayne County's 4th District, which was two-thirds Black and one-third white. Campaigning together helped solidify friendships and promote understanding between Black and white Democratic delegates. Reverend Dade got Downs into Black churches."[3] Trade Union Leader Conference (TULC) member Elliott got Downs into trade union leadership meetings which were only open to Blacks at the time. Downs reciprocated by getting Elliott into predominately white union meetings. Democrats were in good hands with Downs as a vice president and Hart as the Democratic caucus chair. The recognized leaders of the resurgence of the Democratic party in Michigan under former governor G. Mennen Williams were also civil rights advocates.

Con-Con's second day was even shorter than the first, but not for Donnelly, Hart, Judd and the twelve other delegates who had been appointed to the committee on permanent organization and rules the day before. The committee had met all morning trying to set up the structure and rules under which the convention would operate.[4]

Committees

Con-Con would operate much like a unicameral legislature. It would have one set of committees and would meet as one body.[5] Hart and Downs agreed that one of the best ways to deal with young Dems who challenged their labor-Democratic leadership was to put them in positions of power. They placed one of their young critics in a leadership role as chairman of the Democratic Committee on Committees.[6]

On Con-Con's second day, delegates approved the establishment of nine substantive and four operational committees as recommended by the permanent organization and rules committee.[7] The substantive committees were

1. Committee on declaration of rights, suffrage and elections
2. Committee on legislative organization
3. Committee on legislative powers
4. Committee on executive branch
5. Committee on judicial branch
6. Committee on finance and taxation
7. Committee on local government
8. Committee on education
9. Committee on miscellaneous provisions and schedule

The operational committees were

1. Committee on style and drafting
2. Committee on administration
3. Committee on public information
4. Committee on rules and resolutions

Substantive committees dealt with actual constitutional revision. Operational committees were concerned with the day-to-day operations of the convention. Delegates were asked to write down their four choices for committee assignments.[8] Before adjourning, President Stephen Nisbet suggested that delegates read the Citizens Research Council publication

"A Comparative Analysis of the Michigan Constitution" over the long weekend. When the convention adjourned at 3:10 p.m., most delegates left Lansing for a five-day weekend. Conklin rushed home to be with her children and husband Arthur. She and Arthur had considered renting a house in Lansing so that the family could be together, but it now looked like her family would stay in Livonia and she would stay at the Jack Tar Hotel where many of the delegates were staying. It would be a big adjustment for her family. With the exception of Katherine Cushman who had a sixteen-year-old daughter at home, Conklin was the only female delegate with school-aged children. She would rely heavily on her seventeen-year-old daughter to manage the household in her absence and keep an eye on Conklin's fourteen- and ten-year-old sons.

Donnelly, Hart, Judd and the other permanent organization and rules committee members stayed in Lansing to review the convention rules proposed by the Constitutional Convention Preparatory Commission so that their chairman could make recommendations to the entire convention when it reconvened on Monday night.[9] Judd liked working with Hart, whom she found to be intelligent and charming. It was evident that Hart was respected and revered by the Democratic delegates. Judd thought of the male Democratic delegates as "Adelaide's boys."[10] One almost had the sense that Adelaide's boys would have hoisted Hart on their shoulders and paraded her into Constitution Hall if they could have. They affectionately called Hart "Den Mother."

Delegate Proposals

Most of the delegates lacked legislative experience and needed help drafting proposals. Elliott was all ears as convention secretary Fred Chase explained how delegates could get a proposal before the convention. Chase made the process sound simple. All delegates had to do was to take their idea to the head of research and tell him, or the research assistant assigned to their idea, that they wanted a proposal to amend the constitution. Elliott was relieved to hear that proposals could either be offered as simple ideas or as detailed writings. Delegate proposals could be introduced simply by reading the title from the rostrum. The presiding officer that day would then refer the proposal to the appropriate committee. Then the assigned committee would hold meetings on the proposal and invite the proposal sponsor(s) to discuss the proposal. The committee might also invite interested parties or hold hearings on the proposal. "They will do everything in their power to get at exactly what you want to have done and get it done in the best possible shape for presentation to this convention," Chase assured delegates.[11]

Chase then explained the differences between delegate and committee proposals. He explained that once a delegate proposal was referred to a committee, it ceased to exist. It would either be incorporated into a committee proposal or dropped. The committee proposal might—or might not—include the exact language of the delegate proposal. Delegate proposals would start with the number 1001. Committee proposals would start with the number 1. The sequence in which delegate proposals were filed with the secretary would determine their number. The sequence in which committee proposals were reported out to the convention would determine their number.

Continuing to simplify convention procedure, Chase next explained what *committee of the whole* meant: "It is just what its name says it is, a committee of the whole convention."[12] Hart was happy to hear Chase say that the purpose of committee of the whole was to allow free, open and unlimited debate. As the minority party, Hart knew that Democrats would have to fight to be heard and get their positions on the record. Committee of the whole would let delegates talk and offer amendments as many times as they wanted. Unlimited debate would ensure freely and thoroughly discussed issues. It was an informal way for delegates to perfect proposals. It would also slow down the convention considerably.

Elliott introduced one of the first delegate proposals. Delegate Proposal 1010 was a "proposal relating to the equal protection of laws and prohibiting discrimination in civil rights."[13] Elliott's proposal sought to add a new section to the constitution's Declaration of Rights article. Of the many rights enumerated in Article II of the 1908 Michigan Constitution, equal protection of the laws and freedom from discrimination were not among them. Elliott also introduced three proposals pertaining to search and seizure.

Many delegates had deep feelings about the proposals they introduced or cosponsored. Ruth Butler's proposal for the nonpartisan election for Michigan College of Mining and Technology's board of control was very personal.[14] Her late husband Jesse had been a graduate and employee. When the couple was dating, Jesse took her to the college's Sigma Rho fraternity dances. After they married, Jesse worked in the college's math department and later as a campus engineer. During those years, Butler was very active in college life and was a president of the faculty women's club.[15] The college's board was currently appointed by the governor.[16]

Lillian Hatcher felt very strongly that the voting age should be reduced from twenty-one to eighteen and introduced a proposal with Detroit teacher Jack Faxon to that effect.[17] Conklin's first delegate proposal would require electors to vote within two years to avoid reregistration, a change she felt was necessary to ensure free and fair elections.[18] Donnelly's first proposal would require the publication of Supreme Court decisions.[19] Donnelly would later introduce a controversial proposal to delete the constitutional status of the office of justice of the peace.[20] Adhering to the League of Women Voters of Michigan platform, Vera Andrus, Cushman and Judd introduced proposals on local government organization and intergovernmental cooperation. Especially important to Andrus was her proposal to establish a board to supervise community and junior colleges.[21] Hart cosponsored a proposal that would earmark funds for schools.[22] She would introduce or cosponsor many more, often with her good friend Downs.

Constitution-Making 101

Delegates understood that updating Michigan's constitution would not be easy. The 1908 constitution had been amended sixty-nine times, giving it a patchwork quality.[23] It needed to be reorganized and modernized to reflect Michigan's transition from an agricultural state to an industrial leader. Significant social changes and major developments in medicine and technology had occurred since the last convention. The 1908 constitution had made little change to Michigan's 1850 constitution. To a large degree, the state was operating under a constitution that was over one hundred years old. Delegate and U of M political science professor James Pollock was asked to give delegates a presentation on what a state constitution should be. Andrus, Hart and Judd were asked to assist him.

Before rattling off the attributes of an ideal state constitution, Pollock stressed that a state constitution wasn't supposed to do everything and should be as brief as possible. It should be readable, understandable, flexible, realistic, logically arranged, consistent and essential. It should only deal with the fundamentals and must preserve the three branches of government. It should grow and not straightjacket the society that it orders. It should stimulate economic growth. It should provide a mechanism of orderly government through which existing laws may be executed and new laws can be adopted. It should not be in violation of the U.S. constitution. Pollock told delegates to always ask: "Why should this be in the constitution?"

Inspired by Pollock's presentation, Judd drafted a new metropolitan government section for her own amusement. As someone who had worked on and written about metropolitan problems for many years, Judd's proposed constitutional changes would provide ideal solutions to the problems facing metropolitan governments. Judd felt that people's myopic thinking about the separate types of local government—city, village, township, school district, county—prevented a sense of unity needed for the government of a metropolitan community. After checking her writing against the constitutional features enumerated by Pollock, particularly that a constitution should be flexible and as brief as possible, Judd's pride of authorship took quite a beating. But the writing exercise was instructive. She clearly saw that there could be no single plan for metropolitan government that would meet the needs of all of Michigan's metropolitan areas. They differed too widely. Judd also felt that no satisfactory form of metropolitan government currently existed. Although many experiments were going on around the country, none had yet proven themselves. And for that reason alone, she believed none should be frozen into the constitution. Judd understood that inventive thinking and action were required to address the growing field of metropolitan problems. "The most we can do, constitution-wise to solve these problems will be to remove the restrictions which prevent change in local government and to provide the authority and freedom for both our State and local governments to invent, to experiment, to modify or improve, or perhaps even to abolish one plan in favor of another," Judd wrote her journal.[24]

Committee Assignments

On the fourth day of the convention, committee assignments were finally announced. Delegates were anxious to learn if they received any of their choices. Female delegates were assigned as follows:

1. Committee on declaration of rights, suffrage and elections (15 members)
   —Ruth Butler
   —Lillian Hatcher
2. Committee on legislative organization (21 members)
3. Committee on legislative powers (15 members)
   —Ella Koeze
4. Committee on executive branch (21 members)
   —Daisy Elliott
   —Adelaide Hart
5. Committee on judicial branch (21 members)
   —Ann Donnelly
   —Marjorie McGowan
6. Committee on finance and taxation (21 members)
7. Committee on local government (27 members)
   —Katherine Cushman
   —Lillian Hatcher
   —Dorothy Judd
8. Committee on education (21 members)
   —Adelaide Hart (second vice chairman)
   —Vera Andrus
   —Anne Conklin

9. Committee on miscellaneous provisions and schedule (15 members)

10. Committee on style and drafting (15 members)

   —Katherine Cushman

11. Committee on administration (15 members)

12. Committee on public information (21 members)

   —Dorothy Judd

13. Committee on rules and resolutions (15 members)

   —Marjorie McGowan (second vice chairman)

   —Ruth Butler

   —Daisy Elliott

Koeze was in shock. She couldn't believe that she hadn't received any of her four committee choices. How could this be? She was the Republican National Committeewoman. To make matters worse, no Republican female delegate received a chairmanship, but two female Democrats had. The fact that Hart and McGowan were given second vice chairmanships was significant. The only chairmanships available to Democrats were second vice chairmanships. Chairmanships and committee assignments were determined on a two-to-one ratio, which reflected the ratio of Republicans to Democrats at the convention. All committee chairmen and first vice chairmen were Republican. On top of that, every Democratic woman received at least two committee assignments while Koeze and several other Republican women were only appointed to one committee. And Democrats Hart and Hatcher were named to two substantive committees that dealt with actual constitutional reform. This was a bitter pill to swallow.

Both Hart and Koeze had achieved prominence within their respective parties. Both had served as vice chairman of their party's state central committee. Like Hart, Koeze started in politics at the grassroots level as a precinct worker in the 1940s. From 1953 to 1957, Koeze served as president of the Republican Women's Federation of Michigan. She had also been a delegate or alternate to four Republican National Conventions. Koeze didn't expect to receive a leadership role at Con-Con like Hart, but she had expected to receive at least one of her four committee choices. She just couldn't understand how Republican women could have been so shortchanged. She needed time to process.

Republican attorney-delegate Richard Kuhn had no trouble finding his voice upon learning that he did not receive one of his committee choices. His criticism of the Republican hierarchy and elites at Con-Con was scathing. Kuhn charged that there were three groups at the convention: Democrats who definitely knew what was going on, Republicans who knew what was going on, and "the rest of us in the Republican party who do not know anything about what's going on." Kuhn told delegates he was a member of the third group and "a victim of this railroading."

Butler chastised both parties for not appointing women to such key committees as legislative organization and administration. (No woman was assigned to the finance and taxation or miscellaneous provisions and schedules committees, either.) The committee on legislative organization was arguably the most important committee because it dealt with legislative apportionment. Although every delegate had an opportunity to vote on proposed apportionment changes when the entire convention met as committee of the whole, the work of the committee on legislative organization would have a far-reaching impact on the convention.[25] Many delegates felt that apportionment was the most important issue and the main reason why voters approved a Con-Con in the first place. The administration committee may have been an operational committee, but the convention could not have functioned without it. It oversaw the administrative and business affairs of the convention, including budget, hiring personnel, printing, distribution of reports and physical arrangements. Rooms for staff and committee meetings needed to be determined. Areas for visitors and the media needed to be designated. The committee also provided guidance to the convention secretary, the sergeant at arms and the director of research in the discharge of their duties.[26] Butler was surprised when reporters surrounded her after the session. She never dreamed her comments would be noticed. In a family letter that she signed "Ruthie with the Truthie," Butler commented on the unexpected attention she received: "It's the truthie that Ruthie better watch her little old long tongue."[27]

Koeze spent the rest of the evening deciding how best to address the situation. The next day she called the first Republican caucus. It may have been the most important action she took at Con-Con. Deemed the "feminist incident," "petticoat revolt" and "war between the sexes," the incident showed early on how differently Republican female and male delegates were treated by their party.[28] Committee assignments were determined by the convention president and three vice presidents. Republican vice presidents Romney and Hutchinson aided President Nisbet in selecting Republicans. Vice President Downs did the same for Democrats. Appointments were also influenced by party leaders. Koeze blamed these influencers in her journal. During the private caucus, Koeze told Republican leaders that Michigan's Republican women would be most concerned about their actions. They listened. The Republican party could ill afford to lose female voters, especially with the gubernatorial election the next year. And the buzz was that Romney could recapture the governor's office for Republicans. Not surprisingly, Romney stepped down as first vice chairman of the public information committee so that Koeze could assume that post. Koeze, Andrus, Conklin and Donnelly were also given second committee assignments. Donnelly was appointed to the miscellaneous provisions and schedules committee. Andrus and Conklin were appointed to the public information committee. Republicans Bert Heideman and Kuhn also received additional committee assignments.

Despite the token chairmanship, Koeze never received one of her committee choices. The committees on finance and taxation, declaration of rights, suffrage and elections, local government and legislative organization had been her first, second, third and fourth choices. Koeze was convinced that the committee assignments fiasco could have been avoided had all the Republicans, and not just a select few, discussed the assignments beforehand. Koeze's private caucus gave nonelites a forum in which to vent. Many Republicans could not understand why John Hannah (legislative organization and education), D. Hale Brake (local government and finance and taxation), Arthur Elliott (local government and legislative organization) and Alvin Bentley (education and executive branch) received chairmanships *and* two substantive committee assignments. "Some of us felt that if these men would step down from two important substantive committees it would make room for those who didn't get their choice to get on a committee of their choice," Koeze wrote. "The officers refused to consider this." Such party favoritism was unacceptable to Koeze. She vented to her journal that what "teed most Republicans off" about the committee assignments was the fact that the Democrats received their assignments the night before Republicans did, and were thus able "to caucus and make their adjustments amongst themselves." She admonished the Republican leadership for railroading Republicans by giving them their assignments minutes before they had to vote on them. Koeze was also concerned that some of the "so called wheels" did not want to caucus. She understood the importance of giving Republican delegates a private venue in which to vent.

Conklin was also deeply disappointed. She wanted to be on the local government committee more than anything. When Koeze called the caucus, Conklin hoped party leaders would reconsider her request. They did not. Conklin never criticized party leaders. Instead, she complained to a reporter that there should have been a Wayne County Republican on the local government committee. That Wayne County Republican, of course, was herself. Conklin had deep concerns on how metropolitan government would respond to the burgeoning population growth in suburban areas. She wanted to eliminate duplication of government services and inefficiency and worried that these areas could be dominated by Detroit politicians. Koeze felt badly for Conklin and wrote in her journal that Conklin was the only Republican woman who hadn't been taken care of by the extra committee assignments. Conklin was not so sympathetic to Koeze. In what was likely a criticism of Koeze, Conklin told a reporter that she had never seen any problems and that any problems were created by the women themselves. "It's when women go out to do battle with the men, just because the men are men and the women are women, that you have troubles," Conklin said. "When you talk intelligently and sanely with them, they treat you as just another delegate."[29]

Andrus was happy with her assignment to the education committee. As one of the original faculty members of Port Huron Junior College in 1923, Andrus was a fixture in Port Huron's educational history. Andrus chaired the social science department and taught at the college for thirty-seven years.[30] She likely knew more about community colleges than any other delegate and had big plans for revising the constitution's education article. As one of the League of Women Voters leaders at Con-Con, Andrus was also committed to promoting the league's Con-Con platform. The research and organizational skills Andrus, Cushman and

Judd honed over the years as League of Women Voters members would serve them well at Con-Con. Committee assignments were not unlike league study groups where members gained expertise in their assigned areas and made reports and recommendations.

Cushman received two of her requested committee assignments: local government and style and drafting. Finance and taxation had been her first choice.[31] Cushman was eager to utilize her broad knowledge of state, county and local government. Her league-authored handbooks—*Dearborn and Its Government*, *Know Your State* and *Know Your Wayne County Government*—showcased her extensive knowledge and writing skills.[32] The 150-page *Dearborn and Its Government* was still being used as a supplemental text in Dearborn schools.[33] Cushman had chosen the style and drafting committee because she understood the importance of correct wording and punctuation. The committee's basic function was to examine and edit proposals to avoid inaccuracies, repetition, inconsistencies or poor drafting. It had the authority to rephrase or regroup proposed language or sections but lacked authority to change the substance of any proposal referred to it. The committee was greatly aided by convention research staff. Research staff reviewed committee proposals before they were reported to the convention and made suggestions to form, if any. They also examined court interpretations of the existing constitution to understand the meaning behind the language. Cushman was the only female on the fifteen-member attorney-dominated committee.[34]

Donnelly was elated to be among the twenty lawyers appointed to the committee on the judicial branch. The State Bar of Michigan had just held its annual meeting, and attorneys across the state had lots to say about how the constitution's judicial article should be revised. One of the hottest topics concerned the abolishment of the justice of the peace system. The committee assignment offset Donnelly's irritation earlier that day at being stereotyped as a feminist in a *Lansing State Journal* article. The headline declared the thirty-seven-year-old unmarried Donnelly to be a "FEARLESS FEMINIST" because she had questioned the pro-male slant in convention staff descriptions during a meeting of the permanent organization and rules committee.[35] Several of the job descriptions said "he," and a statement relating to research and drafting associates said that "some of these men should be trained in law." Donnelly understood the press' objective to write interesting copy, but the feminist stereotype was getting old. Donnelly also objected to the concept of a women's point of view. When people told her that she thought like a man, she asked them "which man?"[36]

McGowan, like Donnelly, knew she was lucky to be on the twenty-one member judicial branch committee, considering that there were fifty-seven lawyers and a handful of retired judges at Con-Con. McGowan was also grateful to be named second vice chairman of the rules and resolutions committee. Black delegates Richard Austin and Harold Bledsoe had also been given second vice chairmanships. McGowan was also the Democratic caucus secretary. The party certainly was looking out for women and minorities. McGowan was proud to be a Democrat.

Elliott looked forward to working with Hart and William Greene in the executive branch committee. Greene was a Trade Union Leadership Council (TULC) and Detroit NAACP member like Elliott as well as a Coordinating Council on Human Relations and Detroit Urban League member. Elliott was also glad to be on the rules and resolutions committee where McGowan would serve as second vice chairman. Even though she had not been appointed to the committee on declaration of rights, suffrage and elections, Elliott rested easier knowing that Hatcher, Reverend Dade and Detroit attorney and law professor Harold Norris were committee members. Norris had campaigned for Con-Con with Austin and was a strong civil rights supporter. She was especially glad that Norris was named second vice chairman of the rights committee.

Detroit school teacher Hart was confident that she would be able to make important contributions to the education and executive branch committees. As second vice chairman of the education committee, Hart was a de facto member of all education subcommittees. Hart had been appointed by former governor Williams to serve as a delegate to the White House Conference on Education. She was also a past president of the Detroit Federation of Teachers. Hart had learned a lot about the governor's office and the organization of the executive branch from her close association with Williams during his twelve-year reign, and she couldn't wait to put her knowledge and experience to work.

Like Hart, Hatcher was also named to two substantive committees. She was thrilled to be on the declaration of rights committee but not so thrilled to be on the local government committee. Most of the members had much more local government experience than she had.[37] The committee was comprised of current or former mayors, city, township and prosecuting attorneys, a state senator, a state representative, township and county supervisors, a deputy county clerk, county and state treasurers and a township trustee, to name a few. Cushman and Judd would also bring considerable experience and expertise to the committee.

Judd was happy that she and Cushman were both appointed to the local government committee. Both women were considered leaders in local government reform, and both had studied and written on various aspects of local government for the League of Women Voters. Judd's LWVMI booklet, *Our City Government*, was used in local schools and attracted wide interest. Judd was president of the state league from 1927 to 1929. (Cushman would become president of the state league in 1979.[38]) What fun the two would have promoting the league's local government platform! Judd was also pleased to be on the public information committee. She understood the importance of creating interest in the convention, particularly when it came time to sell the proposed new constitution to the public.

Judd was embarrassed that Koeze had called a caucus to complain about committee assignments. She didn't think that women should be given appointments or chairmanships just because they were women.[39] Judd felt women had arrived and that this type of thinking about women in politics was an anachronism. Judd never felt that she was treated as an inferior because of her sex. She believed people were treated as they expected to be treated, and she always expected to be treated as a human being.[40] The incident made Judd recall her 1958 trip to West Germany. She and a group of other women leaders from across the United States had been invited by the West German government to see the new post-war Germany.[41] The four-week information tour was part of an exchange program with the United States, inaugurated in 1952.[42] Judd's German hosts advised her to pay close attention to women's affairs in Germany. Judd later wrote that her heart sank because she wanted to see all of the New Germany, not just women's affairs. She recalled that a women's section had been set up in every department of government, and wondered whether this would lead to equality and integration of women in public and economic life, or whether it would "tend to freeze 'women's affairs' into an isolated world of their own."[43]

Judd exuded self-confidence and a sense of regalness. Her education and opportunities expanded when she was at Vassar College: tea with Eleanor Roosevelt, talks with famed naturist John Burroughs, trips to New York City museums, theatres and concert halls. Judd's larger-than-life grandfather Charles Leonard—whom Judd considered to be the inventor of the refrigerator—also had a tremendous influence on her. After her graduation from Vassar, Grandpa Leonard demonstrated his confidence in her when he listened to her ideas on how to solve his labor problems.[44] He reviewed the company organizational chart with her and spoke to her as if she were the personnel manager.[45] In 1932, Judd and her husband entertained the future prime minister of England, Winston Churchill, in their home. Churchill was in Grand Rapids as part of a speaking tour and gave a lecture at Judd's church. Is it any wonder, then, that Judd believed that *every* woman would be treated as she expected to be or that she would not be deterred in her goals on account of her sex?

University of Michigan graduate Cushman had roots steeped in Dearborn history. She was a fourth generation Dearbornite on both sides of her family tree and the daughter of two pioneering Dearborn families.[46] Snow Road in Dearborn was named after her great-grandfather Dr. Edward Sparrow Snow, and the Snow Woods neighborhood was derived from his name.[47] The illustrious pioneer settled in Dearborn in 1848. Cushman's grandmother Mary Louise Martyn Snow, an early League of Women Voters member, had been a positive and influential role model. Cushman described her grandmother as a writer, historian and a natural student. Grandma Snow wrote for the Dearborn Study Club. "The Snows were always interested in history and keeping records," Cushman told a reporter.[48] Cushman's family history was also closely tied with the history of Christ Episcopal Church of Dearborn. Her great-grandfather Snow was a member of the first vestry of the church in 1870.[49] When Cushman became the first woman to serve on the vestry in 1956, she followed in the footsteps of her great-grandfather, grandfather and father.

Committee Work

With the announcements of committee assignments, the convention started to move from the orientation/planning/operational phase into the committee or study phase. Con-Con operated under the committee system.[50] The backbone of any lawmaking body, whether constitutional or statutory, is the committee structure, membership and leadership. Committees are the work horses of the legislative process.[51] During the committee phase, delegates would spend the majority of their time in committee meetings; studying and researching delegate proposals and their assigned constitutional areas; listening to experts, laypersons, professionals, politicians, businesspeople and special interest groups and holding public hearings. Committee meetings were open to the public, unless otherwise authorized by the convention by a majority of the delegates elected.[52] (No closed committee meetings were ever held, however, and Con-Con proved to be very transparent.)

After the committees completed their work and reported out their committee proposals, the convention then entered the debate phase. During this phase, committee proposals would be read for the first time (First Reading). The entire convention, sitting as committee of the whole, would engage in unlimited debate on committee proposals and amendments to proposals during First Reading. After a proposal had been fully debated and all amendments considered, the proposal would either be adopted or not adopted. Adopted proposals would be referred to the committee on style and drafting.[53] Second Reading would occur when style and drafting returned a committee proposal—with or without suggested modifications—to be read a second time. If the committee proposal was adopted on Second Reading, it would then again be sent to style and drafting. Once style and drafting returned the proposal, it would be read a third time for final passage.[54]

Dorothy Judd's Free Morning

Judd decided to have breakfast in her hotel room. There was so much studying to do! Everyone was studying hard and starting to feel overwhelmed by the piles of reading material. When her waiter brought her breakfast, he asked her what was going on, "Every room I go into is like this. Everybody studying so hard. What is it?"[55]

Judd had a free morning so she decided to walk over to the state Capitol building to talk to the Republican party chairman. It was too lovely a fall day not to walk. Judd was concerned that rural Republicans would try to run Con-Con the way they did the Michigan legislature. She doubted they would succeed. There were just too many delegates who were new to politics and had no political ambitions. She knew these delegates would not be bossed. Still, she wondered if unit rule could force her to vote with the Republican party caucus. The party chairman assured her that would never happen. Being an independent-minded Republican, Judd was relieved by his assurances. Afterwards, Judd remembered that she needed to go to the Social Security office.[56] If she wanted to get paid, she needed a number. Cushman also needed to apply for a Social Security number.[57]

Judd was very impressed with her local government committee chairman's approach to committee work. She thought he was wise not to assign members to subcommittees at the start. Each delegate was given a large loose-leaf binder with one article section from the current constitution at the top of the page. The rest of the page was kept blank for notes. This way committee members would go over each relevant provision of the constitution section by section.[58] While they were doing this, they were instructed that they should also keep a list of problems. Experts would be called in to address the committee once problems were identified. Only then would members begin considering the numerous delegate proposals being referred to their committee. Noncontroversial proposals would be set aside and controversial ones would be assigned to subcommittees. Once proposals were agreed upon, they would be submitted to committee of the whole as committee proposals.

Judd had already reviewed the constitutional provisions on local government and decided that the best thing the committee could do was abolish the whole works and start new. She had received a copy of the report from the governor's Advisory Committee on Local Government the previous day. Judd couldn't help thinking the report was a sign of trouble to come for her committee. The Advisory Committee couldn't reach an agreement, stopped attending meetings and disbanded.[59] Judd felt local government's problem was lack of unity. Separate units of governments—city, village, township, school district, county—lacked the sense of unity required for metropolitan-area government.

During one local government meeting, a discussion evolved into the role of government in preserving natural resources. Because the various units of local government were limited by their respective geographical jurisdictions, committee members felt the question should be handled as a matter of state-wide concern. When Judd suggested that a new article on natural resources be written, she was promptly named chairman of a subcommittee to explore the matter.[60] Cushman was also assigned to the six-member subcommittee.[61] It was a perfect assignment for the two environmentalists. Judd's reverence for nature started as a Camp Fire Girl at the Luther Gulick summer camp in Maine. Judd spent several summers at the camp and later became a camp counselor. Dr. Gulick's philosophy about nature and living in the world were an important part of camp philosophy. Gulick stressed the importance of developing the whole person—mind, body and spirit. Judd's mother also embraced this philosophy and started a Camp Fire Girls movement in Grand Rapids.[62] Informal talks with American naturalist, nature essayist and conservationist John Burroughs during her Vassar years also contributed to Judd's reverence for the environment. Judd felt the students learned more from Burroughs than from many of their professors.[63] Judd was also influenced by her Grandfather Leonard who was instrumental in getting clean drinking water for Grand Rapids residents.

Cushman's reverence for the environment may have been sparked by her Dearborn family roots. She was well aware of her ancestry and ties to the land. In 1817, her maternal great, great-great grandparents Sparrow and Clara Snow moved to Ohio from Massachusetts. They were among the pioneers of the Western Reserve. When their son Dr. Edward Sparrow Snow moved to Michigan in 1848, the "country was covered with forests, and most of the roads were bridle paths through the woods."[64]

Four for Donnelly

Donnelly was assigned to four of the seven miscellaneous provisions and schedule subcommittees: boundaries and seat of government, eminent domain, militia and amendment and revision. She was eager to dig into these areas and make recommendations. Committee members would soon see just how meticulous Donnelly was when she researched an issue!

Community Colleges Spotlighted

Andrus was pleased that community colleges were being spotlighted early on.[65] The Assistant Superintendent of Public Instruction appeared before the education committee on October 26 and gave members copies of the document "Some Facts Concerning Community Colleges in Michigan." Community colleges were the only level of Michigan education that was not a part of the current constitution.[66] Andrus was determined that community colleges should become a part of the new constitution, and receive more funding, autonomy and their own state board.

Starting to Feel at Home

Butler was settling in just fine. On Sundays she went to church. Later in the day Gib would pick her up for a family dinner at his house. Sometimes her landlady would invite her downstairs for dinner. Butler liked her landlady and admired her houseful of beautiful antiques. She also enjoyed contributing to meals. On one occasion she baked apples and made croutons to go with the split pea soup her landlady had made the day before. Butler liked to listen to broadcasts of Michigan State University football games. The broadcasts became personal when Gib and his wife attended the games. "The town will be torn apart tonight," Butler wrote in a family letter after a MSU victory.[67]

Butler felt that many people were going out of their way to make her feel at home. Every Con-Con session began with a prayer, and two male delegates from the committee on permanent organization and rules asked her to give the invocation. As a church historian who had recently compiled information for her church's centennial booklet, Butler especially liked the fact that she would be giving the same prayer that was used to open the 1907 Michigan Constitutional Convention. Although Butler was the first Con-Con woman to give the invocation, she would not be the last.

Elliott was the only other female delegate to lodge in a private residence. Her room at 1113 Kalamazoo was also close to Constitution Hall.[68] Elliott never tired of seeing the huge white iron dome of the Capitol building as she made her way to the Lansing Civic Center. It seemed as though one couldn't walk or drive around downtown Lansing without seeing the stately Capitol building. To Elliott, the dome seemed like a beacon. She knew that one day she would be working inside that building.

Conklin, Hatcher, Koeze and McGowan were enjoying the many amenities at the Jack Tar Hotel. Located at 125 W Michigan Avenue, the hotel was opposite the state Capitol and within walking distance of Constitution Hall. The thirteen-story, three-hundred-room hotel quickly became the go-to place for delegates. Delegates often held breakfast meetings in the hotel's Sugar'n Spice coffee shop, which opened at 7:00 a.m. The hotel's many conference rooms were also being put to good use. The hotel's Fielder Room had a forty-five-foot curving bar. Its grill offered complete food service and featured an ultra-modern Turmix electric grill imported from Switzerland that was said to broil steaks and lobsters in seven minutes and hamburgers and cubed steaks in twenty seconds. And the recently opened Gas Buggy Room served lunch, dinner and cocktails and offered nightly entertainment. Ads for the hotel's newest addition promised to pamper guests with their favorite drinks, fine food and live entertainment.[69] The women appreciated the convenience of its beauty salon as well as the dress, book and gift shops. Time was a cherished commodity and would become more so as convention deadlines and responsibilities increased.

Andrus, Cushman, Donnelly and Judd enjoyed the new Capitol Park Motor Hotel in downtown Lansing. The new unit of 147 rooms had just opened on June 20, 1961, and was connected to the historic Porter Hotel building.[70] Cushman liked to unwind by writing her son who was in his first year at Princeton. She missed her husband and daughter too, but at least was able to see them on weekends. Sometimes they visited her in Lansing. Judd missed her husband Siegal, but she also knew that his successful law firm kept him very busy. She also missed gardening. Judd had discovered a beautiful garden just two blocks from her hotel. The once-private estate was now a public park with one small garden opening up into another clear down to the Grand River. It reminded her of her Vassar College days and made her long to see New England in the fall. Spending hours in the convention library doing research also gave Judd a familiar, comfortable feeling. To her it was fun and like being back in college.[71] Her penchant for research was reflected in a college diary entry about working ten hours in the library on a history project: "I adore doing it. It is so much fun to find old laws and documents—just like hide and seek to try to hunt them up."[72]

Hart had settled in at the Albert Pick Motor Hotel in East Lansing. She enjoyed being close to Michigan State University and its lovely, sweeping campus. The Albert Pick was both close enough to and far enough from Constitution Hall. The rust-colored hotel had an open, rural feeling to it, which appealed to the small-town girl from Saginaw. Situated on two levels, the Albert Pick's 110 rooms stretched out like long arms from either side of the lobby. It was a sharp contrast to the stacked look and feel of downtown Lansing's multi-level hotels.

Con-Con's First Public Hearing

Con-Con's first public hearing was held on October 25 in committee rooms A, B and C of Constitution Hall with an overflow crowd of approximately three hundred people.[73] Representatives of various boards, organizations, commissions, departments and associations spoke on the subject of constitutionally earmarked funds. League of Women Voters of Michigan president Mrs. Irwin Whitaker was among the eighteen speakers. Whitaker told attendees that the league opposed *all* earmarking. Cushman couldn't have agreed more.

Civil Service

Judd and Pollock appeared before the executive branch committee on October 25 to discuss the origins of the civil service merit system movement in Michigan and the findings of their 1936 Civil Service Study Commission on the spoils system.[74] Pollock was regarded as the "father of civil service."[75] But if Pollock was the father of civil service in Michigan, Judd was surely the mother.[76] Judd and Pollock started the merit system movement in Michigan.[77] In 1935, Judd was the only woman appointed by Governor Fitzgerald to the five-member Civil Service Study Commission. Pollock chaired the commission. Judd declined to serve as secretary because she had ideas of her own that she wanted to express, and did not want to merely be the recorder of other people's ideas. Judd recalled that the commission made a long and careful investigation of the spoils system. The spoils system was a type of political nepotism where government jobs were based on political party favors rather than merit. Judd was surprised that many of the delegates had never heard of the spoils system. The Civil Service Act of 1937 resulted from the commission's efforts, but was rendered ineffective in 1939 by a ripper act that eliminated most civil service positions.[78] Afterwards, Judd helped lead the fight to give civil service constitutional status in 1940. The League of Women Voters, with the guidance of Pollock and Lent Upson, were instrumental in getting the constitutional amendment that established the merit system in the civil service.

Dr. Albert Wheeler

For Hatcher, the last day of October was especially memorable. The Coordinating Council on Civil Rights (CCCR) Steering Committee held its October meeting in a conference room at the Jack Tar hotel. Hatcher was a CCCR steering committee member. The venue was undoubtedly chosen to accommodate Governor Swainson and Con-Con delegates. Declaration of rights committee second vice chairman Norris and members Hatcher and Reverend Dade listened attentively as Governor Swainson spoke. Then Norris, Hatcher and Reverend Dade discussed the declaration of rights committee and the civil rights proposals that were currently before it. The meeting got interesting when CCCR member Dr. Albert Wheeler presented his proposal to create a state civil rights commission in the new constitution. Council members were not enthused and expressed concerns that if Con-Con failed to create the commission, efforts to secure civil rights legislation later might be hindered.[79] The Council was more interested in its own civil rights proposal than in Wheeler's. Even Black Con-Con delegates in attendance, Sidney Barthwell and Reverend Dade, were concerned about the proposal's statutory and legislative nature. But Hatcher saw merit to Wheeler's proposal and urged him to introduce it to the convention. She couldn't wait to tell Elliott and the other Black delegates about Wheeler's proposal.

III.

November 1961

October was orientation month. Delegates learned convention procedures, clarified their respective committee duties and continued to get to know one another. October was also the start of the education phase, which would last for the remainder of the year. During this phase delegates scrambled to learn as much as they could in a short amount of time. Learning involved not only becoming familiar with the current Michigan constitution, but also the history behind it. Delegates also considered relevant written materials, publications by special interest groups and witness testimonies at committee meetings and public hearings. Committees weighed all the information before deciding to make any changes to the 1908 constitution. Once a committee proposal was approved in the full committee by majority vote, it would then be reported out to committee of the whole for debate. Amendments could then be offered and the committee proposal would either be adopted or rejected.

The Quiet Ladies

Special interest groups were appearing in Constitution Hall and were required to register as lobbyists. Con-Con wanted to be as transparent as possible. The first lobbyist to register was the League of Women Voters of Michigan.[1] Dorothy Judd felt that the League of Women Voters was the only lobbyist at Con-Con that defended the public interest.[2] Unlike the special interests who only showed up when their area was being discussed, league members were a constant presence at Con-Con. Through their observer's program, teams of league members descended on Constitution Hall each day to listen in on committees, talk to delegates and watch from the galleries. One delegate referred to them as "the quiet ladies" who sat quietly during committee meetings and took notes in notebooks or on the backs of envelopes.[3] Unlike the Michigan Jaycees who stopped taking action once the constitutional convention was called or Citizens for Michigan who refrained from making specific recommendations while Con-Con was in session, the league was a constant presence and critic.[4] The league had disclosed its nine-point platform to delegates in October while the convention was still organizing itself and setting up rules and procedures.[5] In November the league sent delegates its program on local government. Of course, league leaders Vera Andrus, Katherine Cushman and Judd knew where the league stood on local government issues. The league supported home rule for counties and felt that both counties and townships should be offered optional charter plans. The league also wanted a section inserted into the constitution to provide for intergovernmental cooperation.[6] With their conspicuous league badges, their presence could not be denied. Nor could their input. Judd, Andrus and Cushman were secretly proud of the expertise demonstrated by their league sisters who testified before committee hearings.

The league published *A Constitutional Convention Report!* (a.k.a. *Con-Con Report*) semi-monthly during the convention. *Con-Con Report* was similar to the league's *Legislative News* newsletter, which covered proceedings when the Michigan legislature was in session.[7]

Whether or not the lobbyist registration rule was uniformly enforced is unclear. When Ann Donnelly filed a complaint with the fifteen-member all-male administration committee that state highway department and Wayne County Road Commission lobbyists had failed to register with the convention, her request for an investigation was denied. The committee voted to take no action citing a lack of substantiating evidence.[8] Considering Donnelly's stellar reputation within the legal community, wasn't her word sufficient to at least start an investigation?

Deadlines and Feeling Rushed

Delegates were getting anxious. Con-Con's pace had picked up and the mountains of reading material confronting delegates each day was daunting. Delegates were concerned that there was not enough time to study the wealth of material put before them.[9] One attorney-delegate told delegates he couldn't digest all of the reading material because the convention was moving so fast.[10] Even the studious Judd felt that Con-Con required much more concentrated study than she ever put in at Vassar. Judd felt that there was not enough free time to adequately study and that that there were too little stretches of free time long enough to do a real study job.[11] By mid-November Judd stopped recording her thoughts in her journal due to the increasing pace of the convention. In addition to Con-Con study materials, delegates received substantial correspondence from constituents, citizens, organizations and special interest groups. One convention leader's nonpersonal correspondence alone totaled about 320 items from approximately 85 organizations and interest groups.[12] Adelaide Hart asked MSU president John Hannah to arrange for a speed-reading course through MSU's Continuing Education department. Thirty delegates signed up for the course.[13]

Democrats felt Republicans were rushing the convention. Republicans wanted Con-Con to finish its work by March 31 so that the new constitution could be presented to the voters in November 1962 when the gubernatorial election was held. George Romney would likely run. The press was giving Romney lots of coverage. But Republicans also wanted a much better constitution. As the dominant party at the convention, Republicans didn't want to be blamed for producing an inferior document or wasting taxpayer money. Once delegates realized that a complete rewrite of the constitution was necessary, the push to complete work by March 31 ceased. Hart moved to expand the committee meeting schedule to include Monday mornings and Friday afternoons. Hart knew from experience as a school teacher that cramming was not effective.[14]

Delegates cherished weekends home, even if those weekends included speaking engagements and study. Judd wrote her journal, "Back to the grind Monday late. I mold myself right into this Lansing life—and the gay, friendly weekend at home in my garden and with my wonderfully sympathetic and understanding husband becomes once more a dream. Convention life is so crowded in every minute there is little time to integrate one's two selves."[15]

Speaking engagements during the week could be disruptive, as delegates had so much studying to do when committees weren't meeting or the convention was not in session. Judd was frustrated when she had to leave Lansing in the middle of the week to speak to the Grand Rapids PTA. The PTA ladies helped get Judd elected to Con-Con and she couldn't forget the small, civic-minded group. Sometimes delegates were able to arrange a presentation early in their long weekend, as Andrus did when she spoke before the Ladies Library Association on a Thursday night, or when Judd spoke at a high school on a Friday afternoon.[16]

Caucus Leader Adelaide Hart

Under Hart's leadership, Democrats held regularly scheduled caucuses.[17] As vice chairman of the Democratic State Central Committee from 1951 to 1961, Hart was well versed in party thinking on a multitude of issues. She viewed party caucuses as educational affairs: "We have reports, open discussions and occasional advisory votes. The pooling of information gives Democrats some cohesion, a feeling of what's going on elsewhere." She also recognized and respected individual differences.

"I've got strong ideas myself," she said, "but I wouldn't attempt to force them on others." In addition to informing party members about issues scheduled for debate, party caucuses also helped develop party consensus on key issues. In contrast to the poorly attended Republican caucuses, the Democratic caucuses were more effective for party discipline and policy determinations.[18]

Delegate Proposal Deadlines

Delegate proposals continued to roll in. An unrealistic November 22nd deadline was initially set for the introduction of delegate proposals, but later extended to December 1. Like many other delegates, Katherine Cushman was reluctant to impose delegate proposal deadlines. She realized that other new and unexpected substantive areas that required study and action could emerge. That is exactly what happened when the local government committee realized that a new section on natural resources needed to be created. Cushman was excited that she and Judd were assigned to the new subcommittee.[19]

Judd didn't appreciate the scolding she and a dozen or so other Republicans received during a party caucus because they voted to extend the deadline for the introduction of delegate proposals. "What a silly issue to make into a party issue!" Judd wrote in her journal. Judd disagreed that there was some sort of binding promise to stick by the November 22nd deadline. She was heartened that a number of the respected leadership cautioned the "narrow partisans" against making every matter a party issue. The leadership reminded the partisans that they must think first of the public interest of the entire state. "We came here to write a Constitution for Michigan—not to demonstrate the power of the party in the Convention." Judd wrote her journal that some of the Democrats were equally tired of party efforts to solidify them into party votes.[20] Judd was likely including Cushman and Marjorie McGowan among those Democrats. The three women would often find themselves in agreement, and Cushman and McGowan would often cross party lines.

Con-Con 11 Embrace Committee Work

Anne Conklin's disappointment at not being assigned to the local government committee lessened as her enthusiasm for the education committee grew. Conklin was pleased that Alvin Bentley, whose unsuccessful senatorial campaign she had worked on just the year before, chaired the committee. The mother of three school-aged children was interested in education. She had served as a member of her local school board advisory committee. Conklin was also excited to have been chosen to attend the committee's public hearings in the Upper Peninsula at Northern Michigan College in Marquette and at the Michigan College of Mining and Technology in Houghton.

Daisy Elliott appeared before the declaration of rights committee regarding her delegate proposals concerning equal protection of the laws, unreasonable search and seizure and bail, fines, punishment and detention of witnesses.[21] Elliott informed committee members that Michigan made no special provision for civil rights in its constitution as many other state constitutions did. Because Democrat and committee second vice chairman Harold Norris had offered a similar proposal, Elliott felt that he should speak on the subject.[22]

During a declaration of rights committee meeting, Lillian Hatcher suggested—and the committee tentatively agreed—that the word "men" in reference to a jury trial should be changed to "men and women."[23] Unaware of the committee change, Cushman offered Delegate Proposal No. 1442 on November 30 to provide that there shall be no discrimination in jury duty because of sex.[24] Although Michigan women had served on juries for years, the 1908 constitution still read that a jury may consist of "less than twelve men."[25] Cushman was alarmed by a newspaper story she read stating that the Supreme Court in a southern state had upheld a provision that women could be disqualified from jury service merely because they were women.

Andrus, Conklin and Hart were among the twelve education committee members approved to travel to the Upper Peninsula in December for public hearings. Hart was glad that committee member Romney wasn't going. She viewed Romney's know-it-all attitude as rather arrogant, considering that he was a businessman and there were school superintendents and college presidents on the committee.[26] Hart was becoming fond of committee chairman Bentley, whom she felt was a good man and good chairman. She was also pleased that Bentley didn't let Romney take over.

Andrus was proud when the Superintendent of Schools of Port Huron Public Schools appeared before the education committee and recommended that Michigan's junior and community colleges receive greater financial support.[27] The superintendent's testimony helped strengthen her position that junior and community colleges were vital to Michigan's future educational system and, therefore, required greater financial support.

Defining committee jurisdiction presented early challenges for many committees and the committees on legislative powers and miscellaneous provisions and schedules in particular. Controversy developed over the articles relating to corporations, eminent domain and militia.[28] Convention president Stephen Nisbet decided that both committees would have concurrent jurisdiction. Although overlapping of committee jurisdiction was not uncommon, Ella Koeze felt that her committee had been stripped of its jurisdiction to some extent. Because of that, she felt that the legislative powers committee hadn't progressed as far along as other committees.

Donnelly made the papers again for her feminist view. During a committee on miscellaneous provisions and schedule meeting on the militia, Donnelly agreed with a National Guard general who testified that women should be drafted into the National Guard. Donnelly felt that it would be a great way for able-bodied women to support their country in time of emergency.[29] Although Donnelly was gaining a reputation as a feminist, she was also becoming known for her meticulousness. While investigating state boundaries for her subcommittee on boundaries and seat of government, Donnelly noticed that the most recent state highway map incorrectly showed the Michigan city of Menominee to be part of Wisconsin.[30] Her committee chairman told delegates that Donnelly didn't miss very much. "She is really going into this very thoroughly," he told delegates, "even to the extent of finding out what the condition of our state Capitol is."[31]

Seeing her dear friend former governor G. Mennen Williams again was a salve to Hart. Soapy's signature white-and-green polka-dot tie never looked so good.[32] Democratic delegates and Williams's executive office staff honored him at an informal luncheon in the Capitol Park Motor Hotel after he testified before the executive branch committee.[33] A *Detroit Free Press* photo captioned "OLD FRIENDS" captured the great affection between the two.[34]

Delegates were pleased to hear that three professional writers assigned to the public information committee would help any delegate who needed assistance with news releases and brochures to take on speaking engagements.[35] Conscientious delegates who wanted to keep their constituents informed welcomed the news. So did delegates with political aspirations.

Koeze was convinced—at least during the first two months of Con-Con—that she had drawn two lemons. She felt both of her committees lacked an overall plan. "I know it takes time to get going, but how much time?" she wrote her journal. She came to these conclusions after observing other committee meetings, which she often sat in on. Despite a rocky beginning over committee assignments, Koeze relished being a delegate. She wrote in her journal that the convention exceeded her wildest expectations. Although she had had no idea what she was getting into, she quickly realized that the convention was necessary and she grasped her importance and responsibility as a delegate. By mid-November she told reporters that being a Con-Con delegate was a job she would have gladly done for free.

During a local government committee meeting, Cushman and Judd listened attentively as University of Michigan political science professor Arthur Bromage testified regarding his paper "A Municipal and County Home Rule for Michigan." Bromage asked committee members not to set up a system in which Michigan's local governmental units would be competing and fighting with each other over powers and jurisdiction and to leave most of the problems to the legislature, particularly in the tax field.[36] Judd wrote her journal that Bromage's proposals on county home rule were sound and that she would draft a proposal embodying them.[37]

The next day, Judd awoke at six a.m.—as she often did—her mind already racing. Thursdays were her only free mornings and she knew she needed to make the most of her limited free time. As the convention progressed, so did the frequency of meetings and sessions. Heating water for instant coffee, Judd gathered her county home rule materials. She would analyze every critique and proposal. She couldn't decide whether or not to sponsor the Michigan Municipal League's proposal. As she did with metropolitan government, she decided to draft her own county home rule proposal first to know for herself what she wanted to see in it. She looked forward to going home the next day, but knew the type of concentrated work she did in Lansing was not possible at home. "All the delegates are working this way," she wrote her journal. "I wonder how long we will last!"[38]

Education

Conklin and Andrus were both assigned to the subcommittee on higher education, which included governing boards and administrative structure, community colleges and adult education. Andrus was named as chairman of the subcommittee on libraries and other provisions, which included charitable institutions, culture, training schools, trade and vocational schools and the mentally afflicted.

Executive Branch

Elliott and Hart were among several executive branch committee members appointed by chairman John Martin to a newly formed subcommittee on executive reorganization.[39] Elliott had no way of knowing that the subcommittee was exactly where she needed to be. Republican Alvin Bentley was named subcommittee chairman. Hart welcomed the opportunity to work with Bentley on another committee. She and Elliott would grow quite fond of Bentley by the time Con-Con ended. The subcommittee was formed to address consolidation of state departments. Michigan's 126-plus state agencies had become cumbersome State boards, commissions and other agencies had increased over the past twenty to thirty years without a logical structure.[40] Reorganization was a must if the governor were to maintain contact with heads of principal departments and give some direction to the function of state government. There was talk of merging the agencies into twenty principal departments.[41] The 1908 constitution provided no real framework for organization.

Judicial Branch

Lawyers Donnelly and McGowan received their judicial committee subcommittee assignments. Donnelly was named to the subcommittee on courts of original jurisdiction.[42] McGowan was named vice chairman of the subcommittee on inferior court systems.

Legislative Powers

Koeze was assigned to legislative powers subcommittee committee 4, which addressed banking and trust company laws, among other things.[43] Koeze was excited about reviewing banking laws. She wrote in her journal, "This promises to be a red hot issue and I am looking forward to getting into this one."[44]

Local Government

Local government subcommittee assignments had not yet been determined, but Judd was eager to start working on county home rule and metropolitan-area government problems. Judd was frustrated that her natural resources subcommittee had drawn no final conclusions and that she still needed to give a final report to the local government committee.[45] The topic was becoming much more involved than committee members realized and they weren't sure where in the constitution natural resources belonged. Judd was glad that James Pollock had introduced a resolution for a select committee to deal with proposals not presently within the jurisdiction or consideration of any committee.[46] She knew that a new committee on emerging problems would likely be formed and that natural resources would probably be assigned to it. Judd breathed easier after reviewing a League of Women Voters manuscript on Michigan's natural resources. It provided the clarity she was seeking. The paper saved her hours of research and interviews, which her committee would never have had time to conduct. Judd felt the paper was a scholarly document that should have been published. "The League is so modest," she wrote her journal. "The public will never really grasp how great is its contribution to public affairs."[47] The league was ahead of its time by studying water pollution before the situation became critical.[48]

Public Information

Initially, Koeze liked being on the public information committee. She was very interested in arousing citizen interest in the convention and keeping citizens informed. As the dominant party at the convention, Republicans didn't want to be blamed if the proposed new constitution was not ratified by voters. "We must, as delegates, make them understand that what we are doing will have the utmost effect on their future as residents of the state," Koeze wrote in her journal.[49] Koeze was also excited that convention tours would be arranged for school children and civic-minded groups. By late November, however, she seemed less satisfied. She may have felt that she was not given enough to do. Arrangement of speaking engagements for delegates may have been handled by staff. In addition, delegates received most of their speaking invitations directly.[50] Although Koeze chaired the subcommittee on convention hall, her services may also have been underutilized. The purpose of the subcommittee was to work with the sergeant-at-arms and convention guides to assure courteous treatment to convention visitors.

Andrus was—appropriately—named chairman of the schools and colleges subcommittee, as well as a member on convention hall. Conklin was assigned to the subcommittees on newspapers and periodicals and public hearings. Judd was named chairman of the subcommittee on public opinion trends and also named to the subcommittee on civic, labor, fraternal and community groups.[51] Not one to be swayed by titles,

Judd was rather nonchalant about being named chairman of the public opinion trends subcommittee. Judd wrote in her journal, "I proposed this idea—so of course I got the job. Now I don't quite know what to do with it." She was pleased that her new friend, Detroit school teacher Jack Faxon, was on the subcommittee. His plans to invite foreign students studying in Michigan to the convention excited her, as she recalled the wonderful experiences she had in Germany. Judd never forgot what one German man told her during her 1958 visit to West Germany. .[52] He said that if German women had had more to do with political affairs before World War II, they might have prevented the War.[53]

Rule 9

A handful of delegates appeared before the declaration of rights committee on November 15 to explain their proposals. One made the hair stand up on the back of Hatcher's neck. Delegate Proposal 1007 would allow homeowners to own and dispose of their property as they saw fit. There was no doubt in Hatcher's mind that it would also allow homeowners to discriminate when selling their property. The proposal started a long discussion on Rule 9. Rule 9 was a 1960 Michigan Corporation and Securities Commission proposed administrative ruling that prohibited real estate licensees from discriminating on the basis of race, religion or national origin. Although Rule 9 only pertained to licensed real estate brokers and salesmen, many homeowners feared the Rule's potential reach. More than twenty homeowners testified before the committee in support of Delegate Proposal 1007. Committee chairman Pollock also received a number of letters supporting the proposal.[54]

Resolutions

Con-Con's work didn't end when delegates went home for the weekend. Some wrote weekly or periodic newspaper columns to keep their constituents informed. Many gave talks in their communities at local churches and various civic and social organizations. Many were beseeched with questions and suggestions. Elliott and Coleman Young alluded to this in their joint resolution requesting a public hearing in Detroit on the rights of minorities. Resolution 38 cited "intense interest" of Detroit-area residents and "numerous requests from constituents" expressing interest in civil rights and a desire to be heard.[55] They suggested that Detroit hearings be held in Cobo Hall, or a similar large-sized venue, and that Detroit-area residents be given sufficient notice. Black newspapers like the *Michigan Chronicle* and *Detroit Tribune* were weekly papers, and Elliott and Young wanted to make sure that Detroiters received sufficient notice to attend the hearings. Two weeks later, Elliott and Young offered a similar resolution requesting authority and funding for the declaration of rights committee to hold hearings in Detroit.[56] Permission and funding were ultimately granted, and the rights committee scheduled a Detroit hearing for December 18.

Being Thankful

Delegates were scrambling to get their proposals in before Thanksgiving break. When they reconvened on Monday, November 27, there would only be a few days left before the December 1st delegate proposal deadline. Twenty-eight proposals were introduced on November 21, many by Hatcher dealing with equal rights for women and minority groups.[57] Before adjourning at 11:00 a.m. on Wednesday, November 22 for the long Thanksgiving weekend, President Nisbet told delegates they should go home feeling satisfied that they had done a good job thus far.[58] He wished them all a pleasant rest and reminded them that they would be entering the second phase of convention work when they returned on Monday.

Civil Rights Commission

In a November 21st letter from the Coordinating Council on Civil Rights secretary, steering committee members were notified that Con-Con's declaration of rights committee had begun to hear testimony from organizations and individuals on civil rights proposals. They were urged to write Rights chairman Pollock and request an opportunity to appear before his committee. Declaration of rights and CCCR member Hatcher was also very concerned that interested groups and individuals might not have a full opportunity to appear and present their views. When the CCCR Steering Committee held its November meeting a week later at the Jack Tar Hotel, a state civil rights commission was not on their agenda.

Still, the last day of November was an encouraging one for Hatcher and Con-Con's other civil rights advocates. Hatcher and Reverend Malcolm Dade were heartened by MSU president and delegate Hannah's presentation before the declaration of rights committee. As chairman of the U.S. Commission on Civil Rights, Hannah's awareness of discrimination and abuse against African Americans had grown considerably. The commission's December 1960 Detroit hearings had been a real eye opener. Hannah suggested language for a new equal protection and nondiscrimination section in the state constitution that he felt was adequate to address the "whole matter" of civil rights. It was very clear by now that Michigan's new constitution would finally include an equal protection and nondiscrimination clause, as other state constitutions did.

After Hannah's presentation, the general counsel of the NAACP spoke and told committee members that discrimination in Michigan was present in four broad areas—housing, employment, education (below the college level) and law enforcement. He recommended Harold Norris's equal protection/nondiscrimination proposal (Delegate Proposal 1621) as the one best suited to address these areas.[59] Unlike Hannah's more generalized statement of rights, Norris's proposal spelled out the four areas of discrimination.

University of Michigan associate professor Dr. Albert Wheeler was frustrated and infuriated that the subject of a state civil rights commission was not discussed during the November 30th presentations by Hannah and the NAACP General Council before the declaration of rights committee. Although Wheeler agreed that the constitution needed an equal protection and nondiscrimination section, he also felt strongly that a commission was needed to investigate complaints and enforce civil rights. Wheeler was also feeling the deadline pressure. There was only one day left to submit delegate proposals and one to create a state civil rights commission had yet to be submitted. He reached out to Hatcher for help. But with one day to go, could Hatcher get Wheeler's proposal in by 5:00 p.m. on December 1?[60]

"Sex" in the New Equal Protection Clause

Judd couldn't understand why some of the female delegates were circulating a petition to add "sex" to the equal protection and nondiscrimination clause in the new bill of rights section. The female delegates were likely declaration of rights committee members Ruth Butler and Hatcher. Butler and Hatcher would not only be instrumental in getting *sex* included as a protected class in the clause, but they would also become fierce defenders to keep the word in. They couldn't understand why Judd refused to sign the petition. Judd couldn't understand why they wanted her to. "What on earth would we do with more 'equality'! Some women still live in the dark ages," Judd wrote in her journal.[61]

Making Adjustments

It was frustrating not to be able to type late at night, but Judd knew that it disturbed her neighbor, a Democrat.[62] Banging away on her Smith Corona was therapeutic after long, intense convention sessions and committee meetings. Living in a hotel—no matter how nice—had its challenges and limitations. Everyone was drowning in Con Con reading material and correspondence. The extra shelf Koeze had built under her desk in Constitution Hall was insufficient, to say the least. It could hardly contain more than her copy of the Citizen's Research Council's two-volume analysis of the Michigan Constitution, which Koeze found to be an amazing reference book. Trying to maintain clean and orderly living and working spaces was a constant challenge for delegates.

Beauty—Not Brains

Conklin was silent when a delegate announced during a convention session that a woman from Conklin's district was recently named Mrs. America. "I am sure that if a Michigan man had been chosen as the first United States astronaut to explore outer space, it would be noted by this convention," the male delegate stated. He then went on to suggest that Michigan should be acknowledged for its "beautiful and talented women," just as it had been for being the arsenal of democracy during two world wars, putting the world on wheels and for its agriculture and outstanding tourist attractions.[63]

IV.

December 1961

C on-Con began holding Friday sessions on December 1.[1] Not everyone appreciated how hard the delegates were working, especially local merchants. Tavern and restaurant owners had envisioned a boom in business during Con-Con, similar to when the legislature was in session.[2] But that wasn't happening because delegates kept such a tight schedule with day and evening sessions and committee meetings. Instead of exploring Lansing's finer eating establishments, they often opted for the State Office Building cafeteria across the street. One tavern keeper complained that he hadn't taken in enough money to pay for the Con-Con welcome signs. The Jack Tar Hotel, where most of the delegates stayed, was faring better. Its marquee still read "Welcome Constitutional Convention Delegates." But would that change to "Welcome Legislators" when legislators returned in January? Signs that Con-Con delegates were not just legislators rewriting the state constitution were there from the start. Lansing watering holes were virtually deserted in the late hours of Con-Con's Opening Session. Many delegates were actually in their hotel rooms reading material prepared by the Convention Preparatory Commission.[3] *Detroit News* reporter Carl Rudow wrote that Con-Con delegates were considered the hardest-working and most dedicated group seen in or near the Capitol for years, "perhaps since the 1907–08 constitutional convention."[4]

One would think Michigan citizens would be pleased that their elected delegates were working so hard. Yet, despite deadlines, resolutions and the best intentions, Con-Con was behind schedule. Delegates questioned whether Con-Con could complete its work before May 15 when delegate salaries ended. They knew the legislature would never approve funding to continue the convention after that date. Many legislators resented the free media coverage Con-Con delegates were receiving because they feared that delegates would run for their seats. Daisy Elliott certainly intended to. Legislators' fears that Con-Con delegates were after their jobs were not unfounded. Two delegates would be elected to the legislature before Con-Con ended and would have to resign.

Ella Koeze had no political aspirations herself, but she was already getting excited about the November gubernatorial election. Although George Romney announced in early December that he would decide by February 10 if he would seek the governorship, Koeze never doubted that he would. Neither did Adelaide Hart.

Partisan Politics Intensify

Hart was not the least bit surprised by Romney's announcement, she just didn't want him to use Con-Con as a springboard to the governor's office. The day after Romney's announcement, Hart and Tom Downs introduced a resolution requiring any delegate who announced his candidacy for state office to resign from the convention. They said they wanted to prohibit any inevitable conflicts of interest, but Republicans weren't buying it.[5] They denounced the obvious attempt to reign in Romney's political aspirations. There was no need to worry. Given the Republican majority in Con-Con, the resolution went nowhere. The already fragile bipartisanship in Con-Con continued to erode.[6]

A recent attorney general opinion that Con-Con must end by April 1, 1962, in order for the new constitution to be placed on the November 1962 general election ballot had also increased delegate anxiety and divide. A resolution was adopted that would require Con-Con to complete its work by March 31.[7] Under the resolution, all public hearings by substantive committees were to be completed on or before December 21, when Con-Con adjourned for Christmas break—and all substantive committee hearings on delegate proposals were to be completed by January 5, 1962.

Education Committee Holds Hearings in U.P.

On Friday, December 1, Hart called to order the education committee's public hearing at Northern Michigan College in Marquette.[8] Hart was familiar with the Upper Peninsula, having made a tour there in 1953 to promote the Democratic party.[9] Committee chairman Alvin Bentley was unable to attend the morning session, so Hart introduced committee members and other Con-Con delegates who were present. Noncommittee member Ruth Butler wouldn't have missed the hearings for the world. Anything that mattered to the U.P. mattered to her. Butler also had a special relationship with Northern. Her older sister attended the university when it was known as Marquette Normal and was one of its early graduates.[10] Back then, room and board cost $60 a term. Now, Butler's grandson was attending as a freshman. Northern's president, dean of education and associate professor of English testified during the morning session.

Committee members mingled with various U.P. school superintendents and staff during the luncheon session. Vera Andrus was heartened to hear one of the superintendents make the case for more community colleges. As chairman of the subcommittee on libraries and other provisions, she was also all ears when the State Library Consultant for the Upper Peninsula spoke. Andrus's subcommittee also included charitable institutions and institutions for the mentally afflicted, so she took special note of the presentation by the Medical Superintendent of the State Hospital at Newberry. So did Hart.

Hart was a member of the State Mental Health Commission. Her experience with the handicapped, however, started many years before. The daughter of one of her father's best friends was mentally handicapped. Teaching in the Detroit schools also exposed her to many students who exhibited anti-social behavior. Some were depressed, discouraged and frustrated. Hart never forgot a disturbing event she had witnessed at the home for delinquent boys when she saw boys in the school tower expressing their frustration and the look of desperation on the face of one of the boys as he tried to shake loose anything he could find. "It was just awful," she recalled many years later when she was interviewed for the Michigan Political History Society.[11] Hart had also befriended the parents of an institutionalized child. When the institution closed, the parents were frantic to find suitable accommodations for their daughter. The father formed an organization called The Voice for the Mentally Handicapped. Hart joined the organization and worked diligently until a suitable home for the children could be found. She learned a lot about mental health in the process and the incredible sacrifices parents of handicapped children made.

After the hearings, a reception was held for the delegates in the Northland Hotel's Harbour Room.[12] Butler was interviewed for the *Mining Journal*, the predominant daily newspaper of Marquette and the Upper Peninsula. The article was largely devoted to Butler's U.P. family roots and community service. Her grandfather Matthew Gibson and his family were the first white settlers in Republic. Gibson moved his family there in the 1870s from Canada when the Republic Mine opened.[13] When probed about partisan fighting at Con-Con, Butler "insisted" that any arguments were honest probes of issues and not intended to create controversy. She also praised delegates as the most dedicated group of people she had ever been associated with. This sentiment was often expressed by delegates and observers. Butler described Con-Con as the most challenging experience of her life.

On Saturday, December 2, the education committee conducted its public hearing at the Michigan College of Mining and Technology in Houghton. The meeting was called to order at 10:10 a.m. in the Student Union, a place Butler had visited many times. Michigan College of Mining and Technology president Dr. Van Pelt described the nature and objective of the college and recommended that the college be given constitutional status and a name change to the Michigan College of Science and Technology. Van Pelt's requests were echoed by various college and civic representatives. After lunch, the Director of Ironwood Community College spoke about the need for community colleges throughout the state and pointed out their particularly unique functions. He expressed his hope that community colleges would be recognized in the constitution as an important part of the education system. Andrus couldn't have made a better pitch. The afternoon session included a long list of officials and educators speaking on such issues as the State Board of Education, the Superintendent of Public Instruction and the earmarking of funds.

Butler was happy to be back home in Houghton, especially during the start of the holiday season. Butler was crazy for Christmas. How she had missed the scent of the evergreen and cedar trees and that clean, crisp Up North smell. The snow-covered hills of Houghton and its sister city Hancock—across the Keweenaw Waterway—looked like a Currier and Ives Christmas card. To Butler there was no place more beautiful than the Copper Country. Butler hoped delegates would experience the charm of the area and its residents. Maybe then they would think a little deeper before deciding on constitutional changes that would impact U.P. residents.

Delegates *were* charmed by the locals and the area. College officials couldn't have done a better job of entertaining their Con-Con guests if they tried. Maine native Anne Conklin knew all about small-town charm and rural beauty. The intoxicating Up North smell and scenery reminded her of her roots. She was so moved that she offered a resolution to the U.P. citizens for their hospitality and interest when she returned to Con-Con. The resolution expressed friendship and gratitude on behalf of herself and the other committee members and was adopted by the convention. The education committee hearings in Marquette and Houghton were the only Con-Con hearings held in the Upper Peninsula.

Judd/Cushman Natural Resources Proposal Gets a Hearing

Judd, Cushman and several other delegates offered delegate proposals to create a new natural resources article.[14] The proposals were referred to the committee on miscellaneous provisions and schedule. Several days later, the committee held a public hearing on natural resources at the Lansing Civic Center. Ann Donnelly called the hearing to order at 7:30

p.m. Cushman and Judd were thrilled that thirteen witnesses testified, but less thrilled that the hearing ended around midnight.

Hatcher Attends Hearings on Civil Rights

Lillian Hatcher attended the declaration of rights committee public hearings on civil rights in Detroit on December 18 and in Saginaw and Flint on December 19. She was back in Constitution Hall on December 20 for Con-Con's last two sessions before Christmas break. Like the other delegates, Hatcher looked forward to being home for nearly two weeks before the convention reconvened on January 3, 1962. Her youngest daughter was due to deliver her first child in early January, and Hatcher welcomed the extra time home.[15]

Local Government Subcommittees

Local government subcommittees were finally announced to the convention.[16] Judd was appointed as chairman of the subcommittee on county government. She was glad that she had only been named to one subcommittee. Now she could concentrate on county home rule. Hatcher was also relieved to be assigned to only one subcommittee (public utilities). Cushman was assigned to three subcommittees: legislative report, concurrent jurisdiction (Article VIII, Section 5) and metropolitan areas and intergovernmental relations. Cushman was particularly interested in tackling the challenges being faced by growing urban areas. Born in 1916, Cushman saw for herself how the metropolitan Detroit area had become more industrialized and populated. Henry Ford's mass production of automobiles had contributed significantly to the burgeoning population. Americans had been flocking to the Dearborn/Detroit area to seek employment in the auto industry for decades. Cushman understood how increasing industrialization and population impacted metropolitan areas and government. She tried to imagine how metropolitan-area government could meet the problems of roads, parks, water and sewers that were no longer limited to county boundary lines.

Writing a Constitution for the Future

Delegates understood the importance of creating flexible and clear constitutional language, as well as a constitution that would last at least fifty years. They also understood that they could not anticipate everything. The 1908 constitution allowed the governor to convene the legislature elsewhere when the seat of government became dangerous from disease or a common enemy.[17] Although disease and common enemies still posed threats during the early 1960s, radioactive fallout from an accident or nuclear war were more likely concerns. Executive branch Committee Proposal 9 suggested broader language by replacing "from disease or a common enemy" with "from any cause."[18] One delegate felt "from any cause" was too broad a statement. Cushman questioned if the three words were necessary. If the seat of government became dangerous, she reasoned, it would obviously be for a cause. After a brief discussion, the convention unanimously approved the committee proposal and replaced "from disease or a common enemy" with "from any cause." The broader language included possible danger from causes other than disease or threat of enemy attack. Never in their wildest imaginations could delegates have foreseen that "from any cause" might one day include attacks from domestic terrorists. Yet, nearly sixty years after Con-Con ended, armed protestors occupied Michigan's Capitol in April 2020, and armed rioters attacked the Capitol in Washington, D.C., on January 6, 2021. Because delegates had the foresight to use broader language, Article V, Section 16 of the 1963 Michigan Constitution is ready for use by the governor if needed.

We Like Ike

Koeze's earlier run-in with party leaders when committee assignments were announced didn't appear to hurt her any. Two months after the petticoat revolt, Koeze, Hart and the three convention vice presidents were appointed to a special committee to invite former presidents Herbert Hoover, Harry Truman and Dwight "Ike" Eisenhower to address the convention. Only Eisenhower appeared. Koeze was included in the reception group that greeted Eisenhower at the airport. Looking smart in a dark-blue overcoat with a dark-blue and white silk scarf and sporting a gray homburg, Ike's famous charm warmed the crowd of 250 waiting in the December cold to see him.[19] When he arrived at Constitution Hall, Conklin was thrilled to help escort Eisenhower to the rostrum. Ike's presence was electrifying and a much-needed boost to the delegates. He was well received by both political parties.

Koeze was chosen to ask Ike the first question after his address to the convention. Judd was glad when Bentley asked Ike if he thought the federal government could and should return many of its functions to the states, along with additional sources of tax revenue. Quoting Thomas Jefferson, the former president replied that a government that was closest to the people was the best government. Judd agreed. Her recent speech before the Michigan Republican Women's division in Lansing on strengthening state government with less reliance on Washington had been well received, but Judd wasn't fooled by the enthusiastic response. She knew that nobody wanted Washington to run their state but neither did they want to give up their little township and school district prerogatives or offices or pay more taxes so the county and state government could do the jobs instead of Washington. Judd wrote in her journal that she told the women this.[20]

Delegate Proposals

As the last delegate proposals were being introduced and referred to the appropriate committees in early December, committee proposals were starting to be reported out to committee of the whole for debate. President Stephen Nisbet informed delegates that they had completed approximately one-third of their work. Two months after it had begun, Con-Con was entering its second phase.[21]

Local Government

Andrus, Cushman and Judd had been working on local government issues long before Cushman and Judd received their subcommittee assignments.

These issues were an important part of the League of Women Voters of Michigan Con-Con platform and a frequent topic of discussion when the three breakfasted together at the Capitol Park Motor Hotel. Judd had already drafted her own version of an ideal local government section. She and Cushman cosponsored a delegate proposal to "provide for the incorporation and government of cities and villages," and Cushman co-sponsored a proposal to authorize intergovernmental contracts.[22] Andrus and Cushman cosponsored proposals to provide for intergovernmental cooperation and for the organization of local governments.[23] Local government was a highly controversial and complicated area. Perhaps this is why the local government committee had more members appointed to it. With twenty-seven members, it was Con-Con's largest committee.

Equal Protection/Nondiscrimination

Hatcher joined Democrats Downs, Hart, Melvin Nord, Harold Norris, William Pellow and Frank Perlich to offer Delegate Proposal 1621, an equal protection and discrimination proposal that spelled out the major areas of discrimination.[24] Although the proposal did not include sex as a protected class, it was the proposal that the NAACP general counsel had recommended during his November 30th presentation before the declaration of rights committee as the one best suited to address the main areas of discrimination (housing, employment, education and law enforcement). Hatcher supported Delegate Proposal 1621 *or* a nondiscrimination clause that included sex as a protected class.

Education

Butler cosponsored a proposal to change the name of the Michigan College of Mining and Technology to the Michigan College of Science and Technology. Butler told delegates that the college's name was misleading. She explained that the school had started out as a mining school, but that mining was now the college's smallest department.[25] She also pointed out that college officials preferred the name change.[26] (In 1964, the name would be officially changed to Michigan Technical University and commonly referred to as Michigan Tech.) The proposal would also establish a governing board as the successor to the board of control.[27]

Andrus was delighted that two community college proposals were introduced. One would make the legislature responsible for establishing and supporting community colleges.[28] The other would establish a board to supervise community and junior colleges.[29]

Cushman Pushes for Nonpartisan Election of Con-Con Delegates

One of Katherine Cushman's first delegate proposals would require nonpartisan Con-Con delegate elections. Cushman, Andrus, Ann Donnelly, Judd, Marjorie McGowan and Romney strongly believed that Con-Con delegates should run on a nonpartisan basis. Anne Conklin did not believe that there was any such thing as a nonpartisan, and that Con-Con would end up with the same delegates, regardless of whether or not they ran on a partisan or nonpartisan basis.[30] Conklin held the majority view and efforts to elect future delegates on a nonpartisan basis would be soundly defeated.

Daisy Won't Tell, but She Will Propose!

Over fifty delegate proposals were introduced on December 15. Convention secretary Fred Chase informed delegates that research and drafting had completed all of the delegate proposals that were filed by the December 1st deadline. Delegates were anxious to have all delegate proposals introduced before December 21, the last session day before Christmas break.

Elliott introduced more delegate proposals than any other delegate. Elliott offered, either individually or jointly, 103 of the 830 delegate proposals. One delegate quipped, "Daisy won't tell, but she will propose!" The pun caught on. The quip may have been a play on words from a 1913 song that warned men not to take girls walking that weren't named Daisy, unless they wanted to get married or sued. "Always take a girl named Daisy cause daisies won't tell. But she will propose presumably meant that Elliott would propose (i.e., introduce) delegate proposals.

"Daisy won't tell" could have been a double entendre relating to the song, but also implying that Elliott wouldn't disclose the sources behind her numerous proposals. It was not unusual for delegates to craft proposals together or offer proposals written by other people, organizations or political parties. Constituents also pressured delegates to introduce proposals. Elliott was obviously influenced by civil rights activists and organizations as well as the Democratic party. Dr. Albert Wheeler's proposal to create a civil rights commission was a good example of how nondelegates influenced Con-Con's work.

Elliott likely didn't receive any kudos for introducing the most delegate proposals. Some delegates like James Pollock questioned the value of certain proposals.[31] Republican Koeze didn't think most delegate proposals were worth the paper they were written on.[32] Koeze's committee had to review more delegate proposals than any other committee. Of the 830 delegate proposals submitted, the legislative powers committee received 147 for review. Proposals took up a great deal of time and study. They were also costly. Delegate proposals consumed nearly one million sheets of paper and were a significant expense. The *Lansing State Journal* reported that "some proposals came in as many as 10 or more times with no or only slight variations."[33] Granted, some of Elliott's proposals were virtual duplications, but the average Con-Con delegate had little, if any, lawmaking experience. Delegates also unknowingly submitted proposals similar to other delegate proposals.

Democrats submitted more delegate proposals than Republicans.[34] Proposals were a convenient way for the minority party to get their views on the record. For Elliott, the proposals were a way to advance civil rights and advocate for the disadvantaged. The range of her proposals was immense. Declaration of rights committee chairman Pollock presumably had Elliott in mind when he later wrote in his book *Making Michigan's New Constitution 1961–62*, "I learned about rights which I never knew existed before; not only the right to work, but the right to eat, and the right to teach, and all kinds of rights which people associated with something in their own minds as being extremely important and which ought to be in the Bill of Rights."[35]

Civil Rights Commission

Wheeler's faith in Hatcher had not been misplaced. She not only managed to get Wheeler's proposal to create a state civil rights commission in before 5:00 p.m. on December 1, but she also enlisted many of the Black delegates to cosponsor it. On December 5, Hatcher, Elliott, Coleman Young, Reverend Malcolm Dade, Edward Douglas and Raymond Murphy offered Delegate Proposal 1522 to the convention. Delegate Proposal 1522 was a two-sentence general statement creating the commission. The same delegates (minus Douglas) offered a second proposal—Delegate Proposal 1523—which spelled out the concept of the commission, including its makeup, duties and powers.[36] The proposals were referred to the executive branch committee. Elliott and Hart were happy that the proposals had been referred to their committee.

The next day, Democrats Downs, William Greene, Hart, William Marshall and Harold Norris joined Hatcher, Elliott, Reverend Dade, Douglas, Murphy and Young to offer a third proposal to establish a state civil rights commission. Like Delegate Proposal 1523, Delegate Proposal 1569 spelled out the makeup, duties and powers of the commission.[37] The main difference, however, was that Delegate Proposal 1569 provided that the legislature would create the commission, whereas under Delegate Proposal 1523 the commission would be self-executing. It would automatically be created by the constitution. The proposal was also referred to the executive branch committee.

Many delegates were surprised that the issue of a state civil rights commission was referred to the executive branch and not the declaration of rights committee. After all, the commission would be tasked with the responsibility of investigating discrimination complaints and enforcing civil rights. Rights committee chairman Pollock, however, did not feel that such a commission belonged in the constitution. Pollock, like many delegates, felt the commission was statutory in nature and should be created by the legislature. Considering that Pollock was instrumental in getting the constitutional amendment that established the merit system in the civil service passed in 1940, his reasoning seemed rather disingenuous. Additionally, the civil service commission—like the civil rights commission—was created to fight job discrimination. Prior to 1940, the spoils, or patronage, system was rampant in Michigan. Many government workers received jobs based on political party patronage rather than qualification. The state civil service section in Michigan's constitution sought to ensure appointments and promotions based on qualifications and prevent removals or demotions based on partisan, racial, or religious considerations.

Rule 9

Delegate Proposal 1007—which would allow homeowners to sell their property to whomever they chose—was drawing condemnation from civil rights organizations. Hatcher was pleased that her employer, the UAW, called the proposal a shocking attempt by bigots to deny equal protection of the laws to all persons. The Coordinating Council on Civil Rights, of which Hatcher was a member, declared that Delegate Proposal 1007 would reverse Michigan's policy of abolishing discrimination and "seriously damage the reputation and influence of the United States in its role as a leader of the free world."[38] Hatcher hoped that her declaration of rights committee would see the proposal for what it was and not approve it.

Home for the Holidays

On Con-Con's last day before Christmas break, Elliott was appointed to the newly formed committee on emerging problems.[39] She was now on three committees.

Hatcher looked forward to being home with her family. There was so much to share with her husband John. The two trade unionists never tired of talking about the labor movement, and she knew John would want to hear all about the convention, especially in the areas of women's and civil rights.[40] It was hard to remember a time when the couple wasn't fighting for the rights of minorities or the disadvantaged and downtrodden. Hatcher supported John when he was involved in the 1937 Chrysler sit-down strike.[41] Many nights she applied baking soda to his back to ease the burning he incurred working long hours in intense heat feeding the paint shop ovens.[42] John had always been proud and supportive of Hatcher. He encouraged and guided her in her fight to join the union and become a riveter in the 1940s. And he never discouraged her from union activity, even if it meant Sunday meetings or traveling out of town. The couple arranged their shifts so that one of them would always be home with the children. John was also a pioneer in the labor movement, having risen from factory worker to steward committeeman to becoming the first Black financial secretary to UAW Local 7. He was one of the first Black officers of a UAW local.[43]

Many delegates planned to spend much of their holiday break working in their home districts. Cushman told a reporter that speaking engagements, correspondence and research work would be the main items on her holiday agenda. Cushman was proving the skeptics wrong. Even before the convention began, Democrats feared she might become Romney's puppet. One newspaper went so far as to state that AMC would have a voice on both the Republican and Democratic sides.[44] But Cushman quickly established herself as an independent who voted her convictions rather than along party lines. Detroit delegate Richard Austin—who would become Michigan's first Black and longest serving secretary of state—praised Cushman for being the one great independent at the convention.[45] Cushman was among a small group of delegates whose ideas on constitutional reform tended toward ideal solutions to state problems. Judd and McGowan were the other two females in this group that were sometimes regarded as doctrinaire and academic as well as idealistic.[46] But where Cushman seemed to earn more respect from Democrats as the convention went on, the opposite could be said of McGowan. Democrats became increasingly critical the more she crossed party lines and voted with Republicans. Black Detroiters would feel betrayed when she voted her conscience on the search and seizure provision in the declaration of rights article in January.

V

January 1962

t was a new year, but to delegates it was feeling a lot like the one they had just left behind. Holiday vacation was over. Delegates were soon immersed in convention work once again.

Search and Seizure

Con-Con's first full week of the new year was devoted to the declaration of rights article—Article II in the 1908 constitution. Committee Proposal 15 was read to the convention for the first time on January 8.[1] After months of scrutinizing the twenty-two sections of Article II known as the bill of rights, declaration of rights committee members knew that Section 10 on search and seizure would be the most problematic. It certainly had been for the committee. The committee had been divided on whether or not the proviso language that was added to the section by amendments in 1936 and 1952 should be modified, deleted or retained. Prior to the amendments, Section 10 had not been controversial. The prior language mirrored the Fourth Amendment of the U.S. Constitution:

> Searches and Seizures. Sec. 10. The person, houses, papers and possessions of every person shall be secure from unreasonable searches and seizures. No warrant to search any place or to seize any person or things shall issue without describing them, nor without probable cause, supported by oath or affirmation.[2]

The provisos allowed into evidence a long list of dangerous weapons seized by police outside the curtilage of a home:

> Searches and Seizures. Sec. 10. The person, houses, papers and possessions of every person shall be secure from unreasonable searches and seizures. No warrant to search any place or to seize any person or things shall issue without describing them, nor without probable cause, supported by oath or affirmation: Provided, however, That the provisions of this section shall not be construed to bar from evidence in any court of criminal jurisdiction, or in any criminal proceeding held before any magistrate or justice of the peace, [any narcotic drug or drugs,] any firearm, rifle, pistol, revolver, automatic pistol, machine gun, bomb, bomb shell, explosive, blackjack, slungshot, billy, metallic knuckles, gas-ejecting device, or any other dangerous weapon or thing, seized by any peace officer outside the curtilage of any dwelling house in this state.

Two camps emerged, largely along party lines. Fueled by fears about the growing crime and illegal drug rates, one camp felt that the provisos were needed to combat crime. Although the other camp shared the same fears and concerns, the right to privacy was sacrosanct to them. They also felt that a recent U.S. Supreme Court decision made the proviso language unconstitutional.[3]

Black people felt that the provisos targeted them and violated their civil rights. Random searches and abuse by police against minorities was a pressing problem. Police officer and Black delegate William Greene told delegates that he had been unreasonably searched six times in the last decade. Black delegate and successful businessman Sidney Barthwell told delegates that police had searched him so many times he just expected it.[4]

Marjorie McGowan was the only Black delegate who felt that the provisos were needed to combat crime. As a former prosecutor who admitted to being intense about law enforcement, McGowan strongly believed that children and society as a whole were better protected by the provisos. As to their constitutionality, she did not feel that the recent Supreme Court case was on point or that Con-Con should decide the constitutionality of the issue. During one committee of the whole debate, she stressed to delegates that the 1936 and 1952 amendments had been overwhelmingly approved by voters.[5] McGowan's position enraged the Black community and the Democratic party. One reporter wrote that McGowan's stance on search and seizure had shaken Michigan Democrats and that racist police across the country were clipping McGowan's statements and publishing them in police journals and magazines.[6] Some accused her of playing politics. Others noted that she had always been one to speak her mind.

Creating controversy was nothing new for McGowan. In April 1961, she was fired after accusing her boss, the Wayne County Prosecutor, of assessing his assistant prosecuting attorneys 2 percent of their salaries to build a political campaign fund.[7] He denied the allegation.[8] While at Con-Con, McGowan drew sharp criticism when she admitted that she did not stand up to housing discrimination. When she was refused an apartment in Lansing because she was Black, McGowan found another place. She didn't want to live where she was not wanted. McGowan felt that she could have changed the opinion of the people who did not want her there, but didn't try because she thought she could find other places.[9] It was also an isolated incident and McGowan claimed that she personally experienced little discrimination in Lansing.[10]

In what would be her longest and most passionate speech on the convention floor, McGowan adamantly denied deserting her people or party. She also denied that the proviso language was racial or anti-Negro.[11] "We should dismiss the racial question from our thinking," she told delegates. While she acknowledged that Black citizens were still fighting for their rights as U.S. citizens, she encouraged them to think outside the racial box, saying "the time is quickly approaching when negroes must fight more and more for the rights of all good people and put more accent on the obligations which we have as citizens." Her plea that "we must be citizens first and Negroes second" angered Detroit Blacks. In response to those who wondered if she was suffering from an identity crisis, McGowan responded, "I wish to state publicly that I am well aware of the fact that I am a negro; and that I will always be a negro."[12]

Whether or not McGowan was out of touch with reality was debatable. It was clear that she was highly idealistic, sometimes to her own detriment. A statement she made to a reporter about her Detroit school teacher mother shows this sentiment. "If I came home from school fancying a slight because of the color of my skin, she would make me face the truth that whatever had happened was based on my actions and not my complexion."[13]

Ann Donnelly cautioned McGowan and other delegates who thought the proviso language would combat illegal narcotic use that they were deluding themselves. The only way to handle the narcotics problem, Donnelly told delegates, was to remove the profit from it.[14] Donnelly and Harold Bledsoe offered amendments to strike the entire section and substitute it with the Fourth Amendment of the U.S. Constitution— which mirrored Section 10 before the provisos were added—but their amendments were defeated 70 to 62 and 81 to 54.[15]

Donnelly and Lillian Hatcher stressed that the issue was not the rights of police officers, but the rights of citizens. "I think the issue in front of us is the rights of all people . . . versus the right of the police in an attempt to gain evidence and to gain it in an unlawful manner because it is not pursuant to a lawful arrest," said Donnelly. Hatcher cautioned delegates to remember that the real issue was protecting the rights and privileges of the people, not the rights of police officers to "obtain certain illegal properties from individual citizens." Daisy Elliott reminded delegates that the right to be left alone was the right valued most by civilized people.[16]

An attempt was made to separate Section 10 from the declaration of rights' twenty-one-section committee proposal, but failed. Committee Proposal 15 was adopted 112 to 0. A number of delegates abstained from voting. In explaining their yes vote, Elliott, Adelaide Hart, Hatcher and others stated that they still vigorously objected to Section 10 and that they regretted being "forced to vote for a package which was 20 parts good and 1 part bad."[17] After twenty-five hours of hotly contested debate, the search and seizure provision adopted by the convention did not differ from the amended 1908 section except for improvement in phraseology. McGowan's defense of the provisos would haunt her throughout the convention and follow her throughout her life.

Equal Protection

Declaration of rights chairman James Pollock introduced his proposal for an equal protection and nondiscrimination clause to the committee on January 11.[18] Hatcher was heartened that the clause included race and gender as protected classes:

> No person shall be denied the equal protection of the laws; nor shall any person be denied the enjoyment of his civil or political rights or be discriminated against in the exercise thereof because of race, religion, sex or national origin. The Legislature shall implement this section by appropriate legislation.

The Power of Punctuation

The importance of correct punctuation became patently clear when declaration of rights committee members reviewed the anti-slavery section in Article II, Section 8 of the 1908 constitution: "Neither slavery nor involuntary servitude, unless for the punishment of crime, shall ever be tolerated in this state." The old punctuation conceivably made slavery permissible as a punishment for crime.[19] The revised clause did not: "Neither slavery, nor involuntary servitude unless for the punishment of crime, shall ever be tolerated in this state."[20]

Natural Resources

As Dorothy Judd had predicted, the matter of natural resources was transferred to the newly formed committee on emerging problems.[21] Judd turned all of her materials over to the committee. She and Katherine Cushman would closely follow the new committee's treatment of the subject. Style and drafting committee member Cushman would scrutinize the wording of the committee proposal before it was reported out to the convention. But before that happened, both women would appear before the committee and weigh in.

County Home Rule

Although the 1908 constitution provided for municipal home rule, it did not allow for county home rule. Local government committee members agreed that there should be a county home rule provision in the new constitution but were divided on how it should be written. Leaguers Vera Andrus, Cushman and Judd felt that people should be able to adopt the form of county government that best met their needs. Cushman and Judd led the fight for county home rule. They were part of a minority that advocated for true or pure county home rule, whereby voters could decide their own form of county government, write their own charter and determine their own county officials. Under the 1908 constitution, all Michigan counties were governed alike, regardless of size, population or other conditions. They had to elect the same county officers and be governed by a county board of supervisors.[22]

After months of intense study, research and debate and feeling the pressure to report out committee proposals to the convention, Judd, Cushman and other local government committee members spent a marathon weekend in Lansing working.[23] After Con-Con's morning session ended on Friday, January 12, committee members spent the afternoon and evening working. They also worked a full Saturday. It is unclear whether or not they met on Sunday, but they put in another full day on Monday before joining the entire convention for the evening session. Much of the weekend deliberations had been devoted to county home rule.

While Cushman slaved away that weekend in the basement of Constitution Hall, Edward Cushman was at the Dearborn Inn helping to organize a new citizens group, the Coordinating Committee for a Sound Constitution. Its two hundred members were composed mainly of independent citizens who were active in the League of Women Voters, Citizens for Michigan and other groups that had called for a constitutional convention.[24] Ed told reporters that their purpose was to follow through and show Con-Con delegates that the people who had backed the convention from the start remained interested and wanted delegates to follow the League of Women Voters platform.[25] Both Cushmans strongly supported the league platform on pure county home rule.[26] Ed blasted the local government committee in late January when it failed to support pure county home rule. He accused the committee of voting "to perpetrate certain existing county offices" and denying local citizens freedom to decide for themselves the kind of government best adapted to their local needs.[27] Ed continued to run Citizens for Michigan while Con-Con was in session, and he followed the convention's every move. He was as passionate about the League of Women Voters' Con-Con platform as his wife, and no one appreciated him more than Cushman.

Miss Mackinac Bridge

Mackinac Bridge tolls were a sore point for U.P. residents. The debate on state borrowing and indebtedness gave Ruth Butler a chance to vent about the tolls:

> For years I have heard about the help to the economy of the upper peninsula that the Mackinac Bridge was going to give. But has it been? Has it helped us? The fees, instead of being decreased, have been increased at least twice. Why not give the Upper Peninsula a toll free access to the rest of the state? The only toll road in the state of Michigan is the Mackinac Bridge. We are paying for it, but paying for it at the cost of the Upper Peninsula economy.[28]

Butler suggested that the subject of Mackinac Bridge refinancing be addressed in a separate proposal. To give delegates an idea of how important the issue was for many U.P. residents, delegate Kent Lundgren told delegates how his Con-Con opponent's campaign platform was largely based on a toll-free bridge.[29] U.P. delegate Clifford Perras gave Lower Peninsula delegates some perspective when he asked them to imagine the state Capitol in the Straits of Mackinac—the geographical center of the state—with the Senate in Mackinac City and the House of Representatives in St. Ignace:

> I am sure that the legislature would soon be impressed by the $3.75 toll charge placed upon each person who attends a conference in southern Michigan. While millions of dollars' worth of toll-free bridges and highways carry our southern compatriots leisurely from meeting to meeting, we not only must travel great distances but also pay a $3.75 fee for the privilege.[30]

Butler was deeply disturbed by one delegate's insensitivity to the financial plight of many U.P. residents. When U.P. delegate William Pellow explained to delegates that the mining industries had caused a severe economic depression in the Upper Peninsula, a Lower Peninsula delegate suggested that U.P. residents relocate for better work opportunities.[31] Butler, whose Upper Peninsula roots spanned four generations, thought about his remark all night. Often one to make her point through humor, Butler told the convention the next day that she had a new plan to help the economically depressed Upper Peninsula:

> I feel that we should secede from Michigan and the nation and set up the United States of Superior. (laughter) As such, we would be a foreign country and be eligible for foreign aid. (laughter and applause) So under those conditions we would get a free bridge and all our financial problems would be over. Thank you. (laughter and applause)[32]

U.P. delegate Lundgren rose to support Butler's statements. President Stephen Nisbet steered the conversation back to more "serious material," but Butler had made her point. Butler and the other U.P.

delegates continued to consider refinancing the Mackinac Bridge in the hopes that the money saved might result in lower tolls.

Rule 9

Hatcher was relieved when the declaration of rights committee voted no on Delegate Proposal 1007, which would allow owners of real property to sell to whomever they wanted. She would have preferred that her committee not approve the proposal because it was discriminatory and not just because it was a "legislative matter."[33] Hatcher, Reverend Dade and committee second vice chairman Harold Norris were among the eleven committee members who opposed the proposal. Three committee members voted to approve it. Butler was absent, but Hatcher was confident that the feisty U.P. septuagenarian would have joined her. It was hard not to like Butler, and Hatcher was finding that Butler was sympathetic to the rights of women and minorities.

Civil Service

When the executive branch committee proposal pertaining to civil service was introduced to committee of the whole on January 18, Judd was heartened to hear committee chairman John Martin praise Michigan's civil service merit system. Judd and Pollock were acknowledged as members of the 1935–36 Civil Service Commission. The commission's 1936 report was summarized and excerpts from Judd's October 25, 1961, testimony before the executive branch committee were quoted.[34]

Judd spoke out when several members of the executive branch committee, in their minority report, proposed to make the rate fixing power of the civil service commission subject to legislative approval. She told delegates that as someone who had the privilege of presiding over the birth of the Michigan merit system, she saw no way in which the legislature could reject, modify or reduce the pay plan without damaging the quality of the state civil service.[35]

Civil Rights Commission

January began and ended on a high note for Dr. Albert Wheeler and his supporters at Con-Con. On January 4, Hatcher appeared before the executive branch committee and testified on behalf of the two delegate proposals that she and Elliott had cosponsored to create a civil rights commission.[36] (Elliott and Hatcher also cosponsored a third civil rights commission proposal with committee members Hart and Willliam Greene.)[37] Hatcher read a prepared statement that was likely drafted in whole or in part by Wheeler. She explained to members that the proposals were originated by Wheeler, a University of Michigan professor, president of the Ann Arbor chapter of the NAACP and a member of the Michigan Coordinating Council on Civil Rights. Obviously not wanting to alienate declaration of rights committee chairman Pollock, who was also an executive branch committee member, Hatcher explained that the rights committee had taken no formal action on Wheeler's proposal because they felt that the proposal came under the jurisdiction of the executive branch committee.

Although Hatcher knew that neither Pollock nor Martin had yet granted Wheeler's request to testify before their respective committees, she diplomatically told members that she was not sure if Wheeler's request to testify had been granted. She asked that Wheeler be given an opportunity to appear before the executive branch committee even though the December 21st deadline on public hearings had passed. Wheeler's appearance, she told committee members, would benefit them as well as the convention.[38]

Three months after he had failed to sell his civil rights commission proposal to the Michigan Coordinating Council on Civil Rights and to numerous naysayers who said it couldn't be done, Wheeler walked into Constitution Hall's Committee Room C on January 31, 1962, to give a prepared statement to the executive branch committee on why a civil rights commission belonged in Michigan's constitution. Committee members were receptive. Martin referred the matter to Alvin Bentley's subcommittee on executive reorganization for further study and report.[39] Elliott was ecstatic that the issue of a civil rights commission was referred to her subcommittee. She could not have imagined it when Con-Con first began. It was just another sign to Elliott that all was possible.

Miss Congeniality

Given her cheerful disposition and bubbling personality, Anne Conklin was popular at Con-Con. One reporter wrote that she was probably the most popular delegate. Republican male delegates started calling her den mother. It was unclear whether or not this was a poke at Democrats who affectionately referred to Adelaide Hart by this moniker, or whether they meant it as a term of endearment for Conklin. Perhaps it was both. Newspapers speculated that Conklin might run for the Michigan legislature and that she was "making noises like a candidate." Conklin herself told the press that she had not made up her mind whether or not she would run.[40]

Gorgeous George

Hart may have been the one to label Con-Con vice president George Romney "Gorgeous George."[41] Handsome, charismatic and distinguished looking, Romney was also an impeccable dresser. It was all too much for the Democrats. Detroit mayor Jerome Cavanaugh and many other Democrats charged the press with trying to promote Romney into the governorship. Hart went further. At a party leadership conference, she charged that Republicans were willing to sacrifice the constitution for a candidate and blamed "Gorgeous George" for most of the partisan problems at the convention. She attacked the press for conspiring to promote Romney and hinted that Democrats might bolt the convention: "We came to write a constitution and not a Republican platform."[42]

Lillian Hatcher's Best Month Ever

January had been a momentous month for Hatcher. Her declaration of rights committee would make history by adding a new section on equal protection and nondiscrimination to the constitution. Wheeler had finally been allowed to testify on behalf of his civil rights commission proposal and the matter had been referred to Bentley's subcommittee for study and report. With Elliott and Hart on the subcommittee, and Bentley's growing support for the commission, Hatcher was confident that the subcommittee would recommend a committee proposal to create the commission. But best of all, another Hatcher grandchild—a grandson—was born during the first week of January.[43]

VI.

February 1962

February may have been the shortest month, but for the delegates it seemed longer. Daily sessions were extended. Monday sessions now started four hours earlier and the remaining session days began at 9:30 a.m. instead of 2:00 p.m. The convention no longer expected to finish its work by March 31. Committee of the whole debate continued to rage (or drone) on longer than expected. MSU president and delegate John Hannah proposed recording the number of minutes that each delegate spoke in the *Daily Journal*.[1] Rules and resolutions chairman Richard Van Dusen felt that much of the excessive talking involved last-minute amendments offered in the heat of debate and suggested a way to get around them. Everyone was concerned and frustrated by the excessive talking in committee of the whole, but were also hesitant to impose arbitrary limitations. Delegates were anxious to reach the Second Reading stage. Third Reading seemed an eternity away. Delegates talked about finishing work at the end of April. Some even predicted that adjournment was more likely in mid-May.[2] Delegates were always mindful that their pay ended May 15.

February also seemed like the coldest month, at least to Lillian Hatcher. Hatcher was no cream puff. Hadn't she worked with union tough guys like Horace Sheffield in cold Chicago hotel rooms to get Black leadership in the UAW?[3] Hadn't she done the dirtier, heavier work previously done by men—but for only half the pay—when she worked in the defense industry during World War II? Her burnishing job required her to work in a cage with other women cleaning spots and scratches off of the material used to make airplanes. Although burnishers wore huge gloves, the chemicals they used sometimes caused skin rashes.[4] No, Hatcher was no complainer, unless she was speaking out against discrimination and unsafe working conditions. But enough was enough. Constitution Hall was freezing. Her hands and feet were freezing. And the air conditioner was running! Colds and flus had been spreading among the delegates for months. Hatcher was constantly getting over one cold after another. Some female delegates wore winter coats inside the auditorium. Hatcher finally spoke up on the convention floor. The women lost the battle of the thermostat, however, because they were outnumbered by male delegates who complained about the hall being too warm if the thermostat was raised. The head of the administration committee apologized to Hatcher for her discomfort, but explained that he received the least number of complaints if he kept the thermostat at 70 degrees.

Romney Makes It Official

George Romney's February 10th announcement that he would run for governor added to the stress and increasing partisanship of delegates. Democrats continued to accuse the press of trying to promote Romney into the governorship.[5] Adelaide Hart was heartened by Democratic secretary of state Jim Hare's letter to president Stephen Nisbet criticizing the convention as a campaign platform for Romney. Hare's solution to remove the constitution from the "storm and fury of the gubernatorial race" was to vote on the new constitution at the 1963 spring election, four months after the November 1962 gubernatorial election.[6] Nisbet disagreed. So, of course, did Republicans.

Civil Rights Commission

Daisy Elliott continued to promote a civil rights commission to anyone who would listen, as well as to fellow members of the executive branch committee who would review the delegate proposals to create the commission. Elliott was grateful that she was lucky enough to be one of the six executive reorganization subcommittee members who would be studying the feasibility of the commission.[7] Subcommittee chairman Alvin Bentley would make a report and recommendation to the full committee after the subcommittee completed its work. Bentley seemed to be in Elliott's corner, but she wasn't taking anything for granted. Bentley was impressed by Elliott's activism. Reverend Malcolm Dade—who had campaigned for Con-Con with Elliott and Tom Downs—was impressed, but not surprised, by her tenacity. Elliott kept Dr. Albert Wheeler advised of her subcommittee's progress to create a civil rights commission proposal. In an unaddressed February 28, 1962, letter, Elliott appeared to inform Wheeler that her subcommittee would be submitting an amendment to create a civil rights commission to the executive branch committee proposal (Committee Proposal 71). "I hope this language will meet with your approval," she wrote.

Con-Con Documentary

Although delegates were used to reporters snapping photos and chronicling their daily actions, it was a little unnerving when Wayne State University's camera crew installed a camera on the podium in Constitution Hall to film them for a documentary. The morning filming session would provide the only direct, head-on view of the delegates at work. The public information committee had arranged for an 8mm documentary to be produced by Wayne State University, Michigan State University and the University of Michigan. The title, *Michigan Can Lead the Way*, was borrowed from President Eisenhower's December 13th address to the convention: "The responsibilities, best exercised by the people of a state, can be returned to them in all fifty states. And Michigan can lead the way." A hungry Ella Koeze hoped the camera wouldn't catch her snacking on an apple. Several of the delegates owned apple orchards. Delegates would often find an apple on their desk when they entered Constitution Hall.

Equal Protection

James Pollock's proposal for an equal protection and nondiscrimination clause was adopted almost verbatim by the declaration of rights committee and reported out to committee of the whole on February 1 as Committee Proposal 26. The proposal would add a new section to Article II:[8]

> No person shall be denied the equal protection of the laws; nor shall any person be denied the enjoyment of his civil or political rights or be discriminated against in the exercise thereof because of race, religion, sex or national origin. The Legislature shall implement this section by appropriate legislation.

Committee Proposal 26 was unanimously passed by committee of the whole on February 2 and referred to style and drafting. Committee first vice-chairman Harold Stevens credited Hatcher and Ruth Butler for inclusion of the word "sex." Stevens told delegates that the committee did not feel it was necessary to specify sex as a protected class, but included it because the ladies wanted it in. "They felt they might be discriminated against as a minority group or as a group," Stevens said.[9]

Miss Community College

Vera Andrus's fellow education committee members regarded her as "Miss Junior College." Her passion for community colleges and their future role in meeting Michigan's higher educational needs was palatable and her expertise evident. Andrus had lived and breathed Port Huron Junior College since becoming one of its first faculty members in 1923. Now called St. Clair County Community College, the college that was once housed in the old high school and whose entire student and faculty population once fit on a single bus, boasted an enrollment of approximately four thousand students in 2023.[10]

Andrus was surprised that many delegates did not understand what a community college was. She explained that they were a rather new institution that were not even thought of when the 1908 constitution was drawn up. Michigan's first junior college, Grand Rapids Junior College, was not even built until 1914. But Andrus explained more than the difference between two-year colleges and four-year universities. She helped delegates understand just how vital community colleges would soon become. Young people, she warned, needed more technical and advanced training to keep up with the times. Employed people needed retraining or additional training. The Baby Boomer generation would soon become of college age and there would not be enough universities or colleges to meet the crushing demand. In 1962, there were only seventeen or eighteen community colleges in Michigan and the existing colleges were already crowded. Andrus sounded the alarm: "The universities will have to build many more buildings. The colleges will not only have to build the classrooms, but the laboratories and the libraries; they will have to build dormitories to house these students." The evidence, she told delegates, showed that there would be forty to fifty community colleges by 1970. She predicted that more students would soon be attending junior and community colleges than all of the four-year institutions combined.[11]

Andrus urged the convention to meet the demand for higher education and training by adopting the education committee's proposal for the establishment and support of junior and community colleges. "Will we do it in the universities where we have to build dormitories . . . or will we take care of them in our local communities?" After listening to Andrus, no one disputed the importance of community and junior colleges. The controversy was whether or not community colleges should have their own state board. The education committee was not unanimous in proposing a separate board. Anne Conklin felt that an enlarged State Board of Education—from four to eight members—would be adequate to oversee the colleges, and that a separate board was not needed. Rather than create a new board, she felt the State Board of Education could set up an advisory committee to study the needs of community colleges if it deemed necessary. Conklin joined several other delegates in filing a minority report to the committee proposal. Their efforts were defeated.

Andrus made a compelling case as she informed delegates that all of the witnesses that appeared before the education committee favored a separate board. Special interests aside, she also relied on a 1958 report by Dr. John Dale Russell who advocated for a separate board. Russell, who was appointed by the legislature to conduct the study, spent nearly two years in Michigan before issuing his report. He felt that there should be many junior colleges in Michigan and that a separate board should determine where they should be located. Andrus also pointed out that a separate board was needed so that colleges could stop fighting against each other. Junior college boards were too busy lobbying legislators and the State Board of Education for funds to properly do their jobs, she told delegates. Dorothy Judd felt that Andrus almost single-handedly won the inclusion of a section assuring attention to community colleges as the growing edge of the future in higher education.

Libraries, Arts and Leisure

In supporting the education committee proposal pertaining to the establishment and support of public libraries, Andrus found herself once again in the roll of educator. She explained the history of the section to delegates and pointed out that Michigan had always provided for public libraries in its constitutions. However, many townships did not comply with the constitutional mandate to provide a library because they could not afford to. Although the 1908 constitution provided that penal fines were to be used exclusively to support libraries, Andrus explained that these fines were not always sufficient and some chartered townships were able to divert money to their treasuries rather than to support libraries. Finally, she explained how the committee proposal would rectify the problems. After considerable debate and questioning, the committee proposal on public libraries was adopted. Rather than requiring that each township or city have at least one library, as the 1908 constitution required, the proposed new language simply provided that public libraries would be available to residents, without fixing how or where they should be organized. Penal fines for the support of libraries were continued.

The subcommittee on libraries and other provisions proposed a new section to the constitution's education article pertaining to the arts and recreation. Andrus was alarmed that many Americans did not know how to make good use of their increased leisure time and expressed concerns about the rise in juvenile delinquency. As automation increased and people worked repetitive, nonstimulating jobs, Andrus understood that the need for healthy and stimulating extracurricular activities would become more important. Committee members also recognized that culture and physical activity, as well as academic enrichment, contributed to a person's overall health. The subcommittee proposal was adopted by the full committee and introduced to the convention as Committee Proposal 97. The single sentence—"The promotion and development of the arts and recreation shall always be encouraged"—was meant to be a simple statement of encouragement and intent. However, the entire proposal was later stricken and does not appear in the 1963 constitution.

Metropolitan Government

As a member of the subcommittee on metropolitan areas and intergovernmental relations, Katherine Cushman was eager to put her knowledge to work. She realized that new sections on metropolitan government were needed in the constitution and understood that metropolitan-area government was needed to address future problems shared by units of local government. While metropolitan government was not completely new, Cushman told delegates local governments that had already taken steps in that direction realized that they needed a strong metropolitan section in the constitution to help them in their efforts. She explained how Detroit's water system attempted to meet metropolitan problems by supplying water to cities outside of Detroit. Cushman pointed out that when Wayne County started to develop its own water system, it became evident that the duplication of water systems was neither wise nor economical. Cushman cited the Huron River Valley as an example where counties, cities, townships and villages were combining to make the Huron River Valley better by planning how that water would be used for recreation and other purposes: "They did a fine job of planning, but when it came to taking action, they found themselves tremendously handicapped. In fact, they were prohibited under the constitution."[12] Joint agreements improved local government, Cushman told delegates. She cited the creation of Detroit's City-County Building as a good example of city-county collaboration.[13] (A revised broader and more flexible section on metropolitan government appears in Article VII, Section 27 of the 1963 Michigan Constitution.)

Intergovernmental Cooperation

Cushman understood that as the population increased, so did the need for more services and units of government. Because governmental units could get into each other's way, Cushman also understood that it would become necessary to develop patterns of coordinated work. The 1908 constitution did not include such provisions. Put more simply, local governments needed to cooperate to avoid duplication and provide services more efficiently. Services that individual governments could not afford to provide on their own would be provided through intergovernmental cooperation agreements with neighboring units of government.[14]

In their local government proposal sent to delegates in early November, the Michigan League of Women Voters asked for a new section to provide for intergovernmental cooperation.[15] Cushman had offered two delegate proposals to that effect.[16] She never stopped working until a new section was approved by the convention. (The new section appears in the 1963 Michigan Constitution in Article VII, Section 28 as Intrastate cooperation.)

County Home Rule

Local government committee chairman Arthur Elliott praised Judd's leadership as chairman of the subcommittee on county government and told delegates that her subcommittee held the greatest number of sessions. "She and her committee worked many long hours when all of us were home in our respective districts, completing their work so that we could have the proper deliberations."[17] County home rule was possibly the most volatile issue addressed by the committee and one of the most controversial issues addressed by the convention. The division in the committee over county home rule became so great and so emotional that delegates were on the verge of losing friendships.[18]

Home rule was granted to cities and villages in the 1908 constitution, but not to counties. The fight for county home rule can be traced at least as far back as 1921, when the Detroit Citizens League and the Grand Rapids Citizens League pressed the legislature to propose a constitutional amendment to grant home rule government to counties. Judd's fight for county home rule can be traced back to the 1930s.[19] In the 1930s and 1940s, four attempts to establish county home rule in Michigan by constitutional amendment failed. The four campaigns for county home rule were largely supported by citizen groups.[20]

Local government committee members generally favored county home rule for voters who wanted it, but not for those who didn't. Committee members were split on how county home rule should be achieved. One group, led by Judd, Cushman and Edward McLogan, wanted voters to choose the type of government they felt was best for their county.[21] They were referred to as the voter's choice group and the Do-Gooders.[22] Judd was considered the spokesperson for Republicans who fought for *true* county home rule. Judd's group wanted voters to decide whether county officials should be elected or appointed and to also determine the number of county officials. Because Michigan counties differed in size and makeup, Judd favored flexibility in setting up county government, rather than a mandatory one-size fits all structure. The other group, led by Republican D. Hale Brake, was referred to as the Three B's (delegates Brake, Peter Buback and Martin Baginski). Brake and a group of Democratic and Republican committee members known as the courthouse gang successfully fought to retain the offices and election of specific county officials.[23] They wanted little or no change to the 1908 constitution and insisted that county officials be elected, even in home rule counties.

Local county officials inundated delegates with telegrams, calls and visits urging them to retain their offices in the constitution, while officials from the Michigan League of Women Voters pushed for true county home rule. Leaguers were encouraged to urge their delegates to support the local government committee members who favored true county home rule. When the local government committee voted to retain the constitutional officers in home rule counties by 14 to 11, Judd and Cushman made no attempt to conceal their disappointment. They vowed to write a minority report and take their fight to the convention floor.

Local Government Committee Compromise

The so-called county home rule compromise, agreed to by sixteen committee members on January 30, was no compromise as far as the ten dissenting members were concerned. Delegate Glenn S. Allen Jr. complained, "We're right back where we don't have county home rule, but Lansing rule." The compromise was an amended version of a proposal originally offered by Judd and McLogan. After the committee adopted the amended version 16 to 10, Judd protested: "I hope we won't any longer identify this as the Judd-McLogan proposal. It's a desecration of our names."[24] Under the compromise, the five county officials would be retained and elected. Although counties could adopt a home rule charter, the legislature would decide the setup and selection of boards of supervisors and would keep the power to limit taxation by counties.

The local government committee proposal on county home rule that was first read to the convention on February 15—Committee Proposal 89—did not include the self-executing feature that Judd, Katherine and Edward Cushman and the League of Women Voters had advocated for. The proposal also retained the county officials mandated by the 1908 constitution. Cushman joined Judd and nine other committee members in filing a minority report to Committee Proposal 89.[25] The Dearborn League of Women Voters expressed its gratitude to Cushman for signing the minority report in a letter to the *Detroit Free Press*.[26] The *Detroit News* had previously recognized Cushman's unwavering advocacy for true county home rule and for her refusal to succumb to party politics in an editorial the week before:

There are delegates still voting their convictions, at no small political cost, like . . . Katherine M. Cushman. . . . The hope of the convention and of the state rest on such delegates as these, who still remember that their prime purpose as delegates is to do their best, not for the party, but for the people.[27]

Judd/Brake Compromise

In a surprise move, Judd joined forces with Brake and local government committee chairman Elliott and offered an amendment to Committee Proposal 89. The Judd/Brake/Elliott compromise drew sharp criticism from some committee members. Some saw it as more of a cop-out than a compromise. Committee member William Ford accused Judd and Brake of shifting a hot potato to the legislature. In a long-impassioned speech, Ford warned that if the legislature couldn't agree on a form of county home rule, there wouldn't be any: "And I suspect that there is a possibility that the legislature will be in no better position to agree on what county home rule should be than we are right now."[28]

Judd agreed to the compromise, although the amendment did not provide for self-executing county home rule because she believed the amendment would gain "wider acceptance in the convention than any other proposal so far offered." Judd genuinely regretted dropping the self-executing feature but felt the many factors that should or should not be included in a charter could be worked out with greater flexibility in the legislature. Without criticizing Judd, Cushman filed an amendment to the Judd/Brake/Elliott amendment. Cushman's amendment was defeated. After a contentious day, the Judd/Brake/Elliott amendment to Committee Proposal 89 was adopted.[29] County home rule underwent additional revision, and the new section appears in the 1963 Michigan Constitution in Article VII, Section 2.

Another major point of contention concerned the board of supervisors and whether it should be retained as the governing body of the county. When Judd emphasized the permissive nature of her group's home rule plan, Brake accused her of wanting to abolish the boards of supervisors to substitute a commission form of county government with three or five people taking the place of all the supervisors. Judd fired off a response to the editor of the *Lansing State Journal*. "Nothing could be further from the truth," she wrote.[30] The issue was not supervisor form versus commissioner form, she explained, but enforced uniformity versus home rule. Requiring all eighty-three Michigan counties to have the same kind of board of supervisors, regardless of population or social and economic character, made no sense, she argued.

Judicial

Whether or not Michigan Supreme Court judges should be elected or appointed caused considerable debate. Not being an attorney, Conklin was hesitant to offer her opinion. As she often did, Conklin got to the heart of the matter: "The real problem before us, if we are honest with ourselves, is how to free our supreme court justices from political pressures."[31] Regarding the strong opposition to having Supreme Court judges appointed, Conklin told delegates that she saw no indication of such opposition in her district: "I honestly believe all that the people want on their bench is an uncontrolled, unbiased judge, not a politician with a vote getting personality."

Hart Discouraged, but Hopeful

Hart admitted that she was quite discouraged. She blamed Republicans for the long debates and accused them of refusing to sit down and solve problems with Democratic leaders. She was deeply concerned that the committees were working too fast. Hart told a reporter that delegates were at the point of a gun and had to make decisions whether they were prepared or not.[32]

Hart was not the only delegate who felt discouraged. Winter gloom, colds and flus and mounting pressures made it difficult to stay positive and focused. Unwelcomed criticism didn't help either. State legislators— Con-Con's harshest critics—were saying that Con-Con was not doing so well after five months of business. Some legislators said Con-Con was unimpressive thus far and a waste of time.

Pray For Us

As anxiety, workload and—in some cases—depression increased among delegates, so did the need to turn their troubles over to a Higher Power. On February 27, delegates adopted Resolution 80, a resolution requesting that religious bodies of the state offer prayers for the success of the convention.[33]

VII

March 1962

A delaide Hart was fed up with the Republican leadership at Con-Con, who she claimed were refusing to discuss controversial issues with Democrats. She was infuriated that some Republican delegates who were willing to meet with Democrats to discuss key issues were discouraged by their own caucus from doing so.[1]

Con-Con Family

Despite the increasing partisanship, Democrats and Republicans held deep affection and respect for convention president Stephen Nisbet and secretary Fred Chase. An adoring Anne Conklin presented a birthday cake to Chase at the start of the March 9th session. The occasion was one of many examples where delegates demonstrated sincere caring for one another. They celebrated good times and offered support during the bad. Chase graciously credited staff members for making him look good, but his praise was not misplaced. As he pointed out, the journal clerk and associate editor had worked seventy-one hours the week before

when proposals were reported out of committee and the rest of the staff
had also put in long hours. Chase also praised delegates for pointing out
mistakes in the journal so that it could be corrected.

Convention staff were deeply appreciated by delegates. Everyone
played a part in helping make the convention run smoother. Con-Con's
pages and guides in their official uniforms were always a welcome sight. The
attractive and bright young men and women looked even brighter in their
flaming red blazers and gray flannel slacks or skirts.[2] Pages quietly delivered
hand-written notes between delegates when Con-Con was in session.

Day of Mutiny

All of the anxiety, stress and resentment of the preceding five months
came to a head on Friday, March 16. Tom Downs started the morning
session by making a motion to adjourn the convention until Monday
morning for a cooling-off period. Downs told delegates that Democrats
were shocked and saddened to read in the morning paper that "the
majority delegates" made a deal to write a constitution without participation by all of the delegates. Downs's motion was defeated 84 to
36 along party lines. All five female Democrats—Katherine Cushman,
Daisy Elliott, Hart, Lillian Hatcher and Marjorie McGowan—voted to
adjourn. All six female Republicans—Vera Andrus, Ruth Butler, Anne
Conklin, Ann Donnelly, Dorothy Judd and Ella Koeze—voted against
the motion. Downs then asked that all Democratic delegates be excused
for the rest of the day.[3] Executive branch committee chairman John
Martin asked Downs to reconsider in light of the amount of work that
still needed to be done.

Hart called George Romney's compromise with the GOP's conserva-
tive rural block a complete sellout. A visibly upset Hatcher told delegates
that it was clear from the newspaper article that the constitution had
already been agreed upon in private and that Democrats might not show
up for future sessions:

> Despite whether we remain in this convention today or any other day, it
> seems as if we are outvoted. . . . Fellow delegates, I have such a full feeling

within me at this moment that I can barely speak as I would like to. So if I pause between my words at times, it will be because I feel that so many things have happened here within the last 48 hours that I can't quite understand as a citizen and as an elected delegate.[4]

Then, as several Democrats had done before her, Hatcher requested to be excused from the convention for the rest of the day. All requests were denied. Several Republicans tried to guilt or embarrass Democrats into staying. Other Republicans supported their right to leave. The situation intensified after a Democratic delegate read part of a letter from a Republican delegate that had been put in his mailbox by mistake.[5] After considerable discussion by both sides, Hart, Hatcher, Downs and several other Democrats were excused for the rest of the day.

League of Women Voters Keep the Pressure On

As they had done from Day 1, the Michigan League of Women Voters continued to tell delegates what they expected in the new constitution and if they felt the delegates were falling short of league objectives. In a March 19 letter to delegates, the state league president advised delegates that she had released the following statement:

League members are deeply concerned over reports of compromises on key provisions of the new constitution. They fall far short of the objective which groups such as ours expect. We hope they are suggested merely to gauge public opinion. Voters called the Con-Con because they wanted an improved constitution. They still do.[6]

Ruth Butler Charms Reporters

At a luncheon party, during which she was acclaimed an exponent of more business for the Mackinac Bridge, Butler was given a specially made hat with a replica of the bridge on top. Other female delegates were also given hats. Koeze's hat was a nod to 1908, when the last constitution was enacted. After lunch, Butler and Koeze entered Constitution Hall wearing their hats to much laughter and applause as Butler announced proudly, "I want everybody to know that I'm Miss Mackinac Bridge." President Nisbet joined in the fun. "Are you sure, Mrs. Butler, this isn't undue pressure on the convention?" Playing along, Butler replied, "I swear it is not."[7] Butler's folksy humor and observations were a welcomed relief as the convention dragged and droned on with weary and often futile oratory. One newspaper reporter enjoyed her quips so much he dedicated an article to her entitled "Some Characters Enliven Con-Con." Butler was able to make feminist comments without being threatening or offending. Reporters described her as motherly and as a delightful, diminutive grandmother. One reporter even wrote that she was not an "embattled feminist."[8] But Butler probably made more feminist comments than any of the other female delegates. Where Donnelly was never able to escape the feminist stereotype, Butler was never seen in that light most likely because of her age and grandmother status.

Gender Differences

While female delegates attended teas, fashion shows and luncheons hosted by the wives of male delegates, male delegates bonded and networked during televised football games at a nearby hotel. Female delegates were not invited to the weekly gatherings by the coaches club.[9] Differences in treatment based on gender not only affected female delegates, but their husbands as well. It does not appear that any sort of social event was ever held specifically for Con-Con husbands. Granted, there were five Con-Con husbands and 128 Con-Con wives. Still, one would think the uniqueness of the situation would have made good copy. But the male-dominated press obviously didn't think so, or could not bring themselves to write about Messieurs Conklin, Hatcher, Judd or Koeze. Most likely interviewing the husbands never entered their minds. Although Edward Cushman was often written about in connection with Citizens for Michigan and the Coordinating Committee for a Sound Constitution, he was recognized more for his association with these groups and his boss Romney than for being Cushman's husband.

Con-Con wives had their own get-togethers. When male delegates were asked after a Con-Con session to remind their wives of an upcoming wives luncheon—which apparently also included female Con-Con delegates—Hatcher asked if the husbands were also invited. The room broke out into laughter. Whether Hatcher meant the male delegates or the husbands of the female delegates, she undoubtedly wanted to make a point. But in 1962, her point probably eluded most delegates. Convention president Nisbet, always a gentleman and diplomat, responded "I understand this is a ladies meeting."[10]

Differences in gender treatment occasionally arose. During one session, a delegate who apparently was always pulling up his pants was presented with a pair of suspenders that needed to be sewn on. A male delegate announced, "We need a lady with some thread and some buttons. Mrs. Butler, would you volunteer?"[11] President Nisbet soon steered delegates back to the business at hand. Butler never responded—at least not on the record.

During a floor debate on earmarking, the acting chair expressed concern that Donnelly had been standing on her feet for a long time waiting to be heard. "I don't like to keep a lady standing so long and Miss Donnelly has been on her feet for a good time," the sixty-three-year-old said. Donnelly thanked him for his concern, but pointed out that men and women both had to follow the same procedures to be heard, and that standing on their feet was the procedure to get recognized. She then returned to the issue being discussed.[12]

Gender-Neutral Language

Septuagenarian Butler may have started the conversation on gender-neutral language at Con-Con. After enduring extensive debate as to how many men should be on the Michigan Supreme Court, Butler asked, "Throughout this discussion they have been saying 7 men, 8 men, 9 men. I wonder if this precludes the idea that there might ever be a woman on the supreme court bench?" Delegates laughed. Several days later, Butler complained when delegates constantly referred to the governor as "he" during discussions on various executive branch committee proposals. "Are we ever going to have a female governor?" Again, delegates laughed. Two male delegates suggested that the term governess be used, which elicited more laughter. Earlier in the convention when a style and drafting committee member pointed out that "he" rather than "the governor" would simplify language and save space, a male delegate quipped, "The only reason I can see for changing the language from 'he' to 'the governor' is that most of us on the committee did not wish to go around referring to Miss Donnelly as 'he' when she becomes governor."[13]

Supporting Butler, Harold Norris offered an amendment to change the word "he" to "the governor." Citing women's advancements and cautioning against taking the proposed language change lightly, Norris expressed his hope that Michigan would one day have a female governor. In opposing Norris's amendment, one delegate cautioned delegates not to forget their English and to remember that "he" included women. He pointed out that although there were women in Congress, there was no official term as "congresswoman." Although Norris's amendment was adopted, style and drafting would later change the language back to "he."[14]

Constitution Rewrite More Than Anyone Bargained For

On Sunday, March 25, the parishioners of Reverend Malcolm Dade's Detroit church offered prayers for delegates and for the convention. Just several weeks earlier, Alvin Bentley and the three convention vice presidents had offered a resolution requesting that religious bodies of the state offer prayers for the success of the convention.[15] Con-Con needed all the prayers it could get. There were only thirty-six more session days before delegate salaries ended. Some delegates threatened to pack up and go home if their pay ended after May 15. Others said they would stay as long as necessary, regardless of money.[16] That was all well and good for delegates who could afford to work without pay. Most of the eleven Con-Con women could. Recently retired Andrus presumably had a pension. Cushman, Conklin, Judd and Koeze had husbands. Hatcher also had a husband who could support her, but it was unlikely that her position as a UAW international representative would be in jeopardy if the convention lasted longer than anticipated. Widowed Butler appeared to be provided for. Attorneys Donnelly and McGowan had their law practices, but Con-Con was already a full-time job. School wouldn't start for another five months, so music teacher Hart was not concerned. Divorced realtor Elliott likely would be affected more than any of the other female delegates if delegate pay ended, but if Elliott was anything she was resourceful. Even if every delegate agreed to work without pay, the lease on Constitution Hall would expire on May 31, and delegates would need to vacate before then so that the Hall could be restored to its former self.

The 1850 convention lasted only seventy-four days. The 1907–8 convention lasted 123 days. March 26 would be day 107 and everyone feared Con-Con would not complete its work by May 15. The only way to continue the convention would be to ask the legislature for more money for salaries, and it was extremely unlikely that legislators would approve the added expense. Legislators had already indicated that they would not give Con-Con all the money it had requested for windup expenses.

Donnelly and McGowan Seek to Eliminate Justice of the Peace System

Elimination of the justice of the peace system was hotly debated at Con-Con. Donnelly had offered a proposal months earlier to delete the constitutional status of the office of justice of the peace. Under Donnelly's proposal, the legislature could either retain justices of the peace or establish other courts of civil and criminal jurisdiction below the Supreme Court, when authorized by a two-thirds vote of the legislature.[17] McGowan also favored the elimination of the antiquated justice of the peace courts "with their questionable" fee systems.[18] In the end, the justice of the peace system was eliminated.[19]

Donnelly Wants All Judges to Be Attorneys

Donnelly also strongly advocated that all judges should be licensed attorneys, no matter how small the court or the monetary compensation involved. "We cannot delegate to the individuals in lesser-populated areas a lesser degree of justice and administration," she told delegates. "Cheap justice," she said, "is worse in many ways than justice delayed or justice denied."[20] Under the 1908 constitution, only Supreme Court and circuit court judges were required to be licensed to practice law in Michigan. Under the 1963 constitution, justices and judges are required to be licensed attorneys.

Con-Con Reviews Five Judicial Reorganization Plans

Another hot topic concerned the method by which judges would be selected. Five state judicial reorganization plans which included suggestions on how judges should be selected were presented to the convention.[21] The Missouri, Black, American Bar Association, current system and combination plans were considered carefully and debated for months.[22] Donnelly felt that people should be able to elect their judges on a non-partisan basis. Many delegates agreed that people should have the right to select the person who was going to sit in judgment of them.

McGowan Wants Supreme Court to Issue Advisory Opinions

McGowan favored a new section in the constitution that would require the Michigan Supreme Court to furnish advisory opinions on important questions of law and on solemn occasions if requested by the governor or either House of the legislature. McGowan explained to delegates that a "solemn occasion" meant a serious and unusual urgent need. Such an urgent need could occur when either branch of the legislature questioned their power and authority to act. McGowan cited the example of the four-cent sales tax which was passed by the legislature but declared unconstitutional a short time later.[23] McGowan also felt the new section would facilitate more effective governmental operations.

McGowan Fights Efforts to Abolish Recorder's Court

Given her history with Detroit's Recorder's Court, it was not surprising that McGowan vowed to fight any attempts to abolish the Court. McGowan claimed the move to abolish the court came from upstate members of the judicial committee who were unfamiliar with the court's work and reputation.[24]

Probate Court

Debate over whether or not the probate court should continue to have exclusive jurisdiction over children was emotional and heated. Michigan's 1908 constitution provided that probate courts had "original jurisdiction in all cases of juvenile delinquents and dependents." Judicial Committee Proposal 94 sought to add a proviso to allow the legislature to create a family court—or other court—if it deemed best. The additional language "except as provided by law" worried delegates like Donnelly who did not trust the legislature and feared that exclusive jurisdiction of juveniles could be taken away from probate courts. Elliott feared the added language would deprive juveniles of the bill of rights. She wanted a guarantee that juveniles would not be tried in adversarial or criminal courts. A trembling Koeze told delegates she was very concerned about the future of her grandchildren. Cushman assured delegates that no one wanted to put children in an adversary position. The intent of the committee proposal, she explained, was to keep the constitution flexible enough to meet future changes. Judd and McGowan echoed Cushman's statements. McGowan stated: "The committee proposal simply gives the legislature the power to determine what court will handle family problems, including the problems of delinquent or dependent children."[25]

Filling Judicial Vacancies

Once again, McGowan broke with her party, this time on eliminating the practice of allowing the governor to fill judicial vacancies. She felt this change would take the politics out of the system and disagreed that it would "keep Negroes off the bench."[26] She felt Blacks had reached a station in society where they could seek judicial posts on their own.

Appellate Court

The creation of an appellate court would prove to be one of Con-Con's greatest achievements. McGowan pointed out that the appellate court would ensure the right of appeal in criminal cases where such a right did not formerly exist. The appellate court was intended to relieve the Supreme Court of some of its appellate load, thereby giving it greater discretion to sift judicial cases and concentrate on those involving more important questions.[27]

Civil Rights Commission

On the evening of March 5, 1962, Elliott, Hart and other executive branch committee members sat in a meeting room in the Lansing YWCA and listened as executive reorganization subcommittee chairman Bentley reported on his committee's work. Elliott and Hart already knew that Bentley would recommend an amendment to executive branch Committee Proposal 71 to create a state civil rights commission. The subcommittee amendment was unanimously adopted by the full committee on a roll call vote.

On March 28, a committee proposal to create a state civil rights commission was finally introduced to the convention. Executive branch committee chairman Martin offered the proposal as a new section "i" to Committee Proposal 71:

> Sec. i. Within 2 years after the adoption of this constitution, the legislature shall establish a civil rights commission within the executive branch to

secure the protection of the civil rights guaranteed by this constitution. In the event the legislature does not establish a civil rights commission during this period, the governor under the provisions of this paragraph shall by executive order establish such a commission.[28]

Interestingly enough, a new section "h"—to create a state highway commission—was offered to Committee Proposal 71 the day before.[29] The state highway commission proposal would fare much better in committee of the whole debates than the civil rights commission proposal.

Statutory Argument

After introducing Committee Proposal 71(i), Martin wasted no time addressing the statutory argument that the commission should be created by the legislature and not in the constitution. Martin agreed that under ordinary circumstances the commission should be created legislatively rather than constitutionally, but given the legislature's repeated failure to act in the area of civil rights, he argued that a constitutionally created commission was justified.

Bentley informed delegates that both his subcommittee and the full committee had approved the amendment with considerable bipartisan support. Under no circumstances, warned Bentley, should the commission ever become a partisan issue. Before yielding the floor to Elliott, the "distinguished delegate from Detroit," Bentley praised her for being a valuable member of both the committee and subcommittee.[30] Elliott, he told delegates, was not only very active in getting the proposal to create the commission before the committee, but also in helping to bring it to fruition. Elliott never forgot how Bentley helped get the civil rights commission proposal before the convention.[31]

Elliott echoed much of Martin's reasoning. "We would not have conceived the idea of requesting constitutional provision for the commission had not the legislature refused to adopt any of the civil rights bills which have been introduced during the past 5 years," she said. Elliott then emphasized that only two weeks prior, a proposed civil rights bill was not even voted out of committee and given the benefit of floor debate, let alone vote.

Delegates voiced their fears about creating a commission:

- that the governor could exercise unbridled power to create a commission if the legislature failed to act,
- that the proposed language could create a quasi-legislative board that would act as prosecutor and jury,
- that the equal protection guarantees and nondiscrimination provision contained in Committee Proposal 26 were sufficient and did not need an administrative board to enforce those rights,
- that the legislature could render a governor-created commission ineffective by failing to allocate sufficient funds to the commission,
- that the commission would not be strictly a fact-finding commission like the federal commission on civil rights,
- that the commission could initiate administrative proceedings and require alleged violators to appear before it.

The two main arguments for and against creating a commission were (1) the *do-nothing legislature* had repeatedly failed to act, and (2) the commission was a legislative matter. These pro and con arguments would volley back and forth throughout the debates like an emotionally charged tennis match.

Delegate, MSU president and chairman of the U.S. Civil Rights Commission John Hannah launched into a historical, emotional and stirring speech on the state of civil rights in American and why the commission must be created. He told delegates that the most significant single domestic problem that the United States faced was decent treatment of minority groups. A deeply moved Elliott told delegates that she thought Hannah's remarks constituted one of the most brilliant speeches on the convention floor.

Hatcher was relieved when Martin quickly addressed arguments that the issue of a civil rights commission should be referred to the declaration of rights committee. Martin stressed that the matter had been discussed with the rights committee and that "it was made clear to us that this was our responsibility and not theirs."

After lunch, Romney made a stirring and deeply personal statement in support of the commission. As a Mormon, Romney told delegates that he was a member of a minority group that knew the longtime harmful effect of persecution and discrimination: "Such persecution prevented my being born in this country and made me at 5 years of age a revolutionary refugee." Extraordinary situations require extraordinary actions, Romney told delegates, and "we have a case of extraordinary injustice that we are dealing with."[32]

The Donnelly Amendment

Debate continued to intensify as amendments were offered. Donnelly's amendment was one of the most controversial: "This provision shall not be construed to enable the denial to any citizen of any direct and immediate legal remedy in the courts of this state."[33]

Donnelly was adamant that the right to trial be preserved. She also expressed concerns that complainants could be forced to go through the commission first before their rights were firmly established. She wanted complainants to be able to immediately take their cases to court if they so desired. Elliott viewed Donnelly's amendment as an attempt to undermine the commission. Although he opposed Donnelly's amendment, Downs expressed concern that it could be misconstrued: "I certainly respect Delegate Donnelly's concern she has shown on the floor repeatedly for the right of individuals to use their legal remedies." Donnelly agreed to have her amendment passed temporarily to give her an opportunity to consider revised language being offered by Martin and other delegates.

The second day of debate on the creation of a state civil rights commission proved even more contentious and lengthy than the first. Many of the same arguments were rehashed and the simple, straightforward committee proposal first introduced by Martin continued to mutate.

Black delegates Richard Austin, Elliott, Coleman Young and three other Democrats offered an amendment—the Austin amendment—which enlarged the commission's membership and set forth in the greatest detail thus far the commission's duties and powers.[34] It also required that the legislature allocate sufficient funds for the efficient operation of the commission. The amendment cosponsors wanted to ensure that the legislature didn't torpedo the new commission by withholding or providing insufficient funds. Austin reminded delegates that the civil service commission and the newly created highway commission had been given constitutional status. He further pointed out that delegates had provided sufficient specificity to make sure that there was no question about what was intended in regard to the duties, powers, terms of office, framework, appointments and political composition of the commission. The civil rights commission was no less deserving of the same specificity. Elliott reminded delegates that the duties and powers of the highway and civil service commissions were spelled out and stressed that a civil rights commission should not be held second to a highway commission or a civil service commission. Elliott reminded delegates that they were dealing with the rights of human beings, which were far more fundamental, far more wide ranging and more subject to emotional and political evaluation than a highway commission. She stressed that human beings, not highways, were in need of a commission.[35]

Concerned that the rights of some people could be violated in the process of protecting the civil rights of other people, Donnelly warned that all the commission needed was one "McCarthy."[36] Like many of the delegates, Donnelly feared constitutionalizing a commission that could have overreaching powers. The McCarthy witch hunt of the 1950s was still fresh in the minds of many Americans. U.S. Senator Joseph McCarthy's allegations that the government, universities and film industry were infiltrated with communists forced many innocent people to appear before the House Un-American Activities Committee to prove their innocence. Numerous careers and reputations were destroyed in the process.

While Donnelly was concerned about potential abuses, she was primarily concerned about preserving the basic right of trial for every citizen. She felt that anyone bringing a discrimination action should be able to go "immediately" to court without first having to exhaust their remedies through an administrative board. Donnelly's experience with the civil service commission obviously influenced her. "I had a certain amount of trouble with the civil service commission in trying to get some redress of grievances there," she told delegates. She complained about having to exhaust her remedies and to take her client back and forth to Lansing. "So I'm not too delighted . . . and I'd like to be able to take them directly to court sometimes."[37]

Various amendments were offered to her amendment. Donnelly became increasingly vociferous the more she advocated for her amendment. "If my memory serves me, this is the third time I have defended this sentence or something similar thereto," an exasperated Donnelly told delegates. After considerable heated debate, the sentence made its way into the final product with few changes. Delegates referred to the sentence as "the last sentence" or the "Donnelly amendment" because it was substantially similar to Donnelly's initial amendment.[38]

Donnelly never objected to the creation of the commission, but she was adamant that citizens should have the option of going to court. Elliott and Young questioned her motives. Young stated that judging from Donnelly's comments there could be no doubt as to what her intention was in tacking on the last sentence. Elliott told delegates that Donnelly's amendment weakened the intent of the proponents of the civil rights commission: "It weakens the powers of the commission by allowing persons to bypass the commission and go directly to court." Black attorney Wynne Garvin did not feel Donnelly intended to weaken the commission, although he felt her amendment would do just that: "I know Miss Donnelly quite well, and apparently this isn't anything she would intentionally do. I understand the reasoning behind it; but I also understand the results." Retired circuit judge Earl Pugsley told delegates that he did not believe that Donnelly's amendment was intended "either in spirit or in form, to any way jeopardize the work of the commission."[39] Pugsley further stated that Donnelly's amendment would be a safeguard and a valuable addition and asset to the commission. Many of Con-Con's attorneys and delegates agreed with him.

At 11:20 p.m., an exhausted and weary convention adjourned until 9:00 a.m. the next day. Any hopes that the convention would wrap up debate on the civil rights commission were soon dashed Friday morning when Republican D. Hale Brake moved that consideration of Committee Proposal 71 be postponed until the afternoon session of Tuesday, April 3. After heated opposition from several Democratic delegates, Brakes's motion was adopted 87 to 44, mostly along party lines.[40]

Deadline Disaster Feared as Con-Con Crawls Along

"Deadline Disaster Feared as Con-Con Crawls Along." The *Detroit News* headline didn't help the already low morale among delegates. Convention president Nisbet felt like he was sitting on a powder keg with a lit fuse. The normally optimistic Nisbet had to admit Con-Con was in trouble. There was no hope for putting the new constitution on the November ballot. Delegates had to face reality. The new constitution would not appear on the ballot before spring 1963.

The rules and resolution committee recommendation that working hours be significantly increased was not welcome news to the already fatigued delegates. Democrat Melvin Nord called the proposed new hours mental torture. Another Democrat complained that Republicans had prolonged debate with their excessive talking.[41] Even rules committee chairman Richard Van Dusen admitted that Republicans were guiltier of long-winded oratory. One delegate noted that delegates had debated 350,000 words above the 2,5000,000 word maximum anticipated when Con-Con began. It was late March and there were thirty-nine articles, thirteen minority reports and twelve exclusion reports still to be debated. And delegates were still on First Reading of proposals. Extensive debate regarding reapportionment of the legislature was expected, especially in light of a recent U.S. Supreme Court decision. The High Court had ordered a Tennessee federal court to hear a voters' suit calling for reapportionment as provided by the state's constitution.

VIII.

April 1962

I t was spring, and the days were getting longer. Con-Con's workload was getting longer. Each day seemed to be a repeat of the one before. Breakfast. Constitution Hall. Lunch. Constitution Hall. Dinner. Constitution Hall. Perhaps it was a good thing that there were no windows in Constitution Hall to lure delegates' attention outside to the changing season. Staying focused and energized was becoming harder and harder. It seemed as though Con-Con would never end.

Apportionment

Delegates spent four hours Monday night, April 2, 1962, debating apportionment. It was obvious that many more hours would be needed. Daisy Elliott and Lillian Hatcher were disappointed that the convention agreed to postpone further consideration of the civil rights commission until action was completed on apportionment (Committee Proposal 80).[1] Apportionment—how members of the state legislature were chosen—was perhaps the most controversial and longest-debated issue at the convention. Ruth Butler had reason to worry. The Upper Peninsula was overrepresented with three Senate and seven House seats. Although Butler was confident that the U.P. would retain its Senate seats, she feared the loss of House seats. The population of the Upper Peninsula represented less than 4 percent of the state.[2] Democrats wanted both Houses redistricted on a strict population basis. Republicans agreed that the House should be based on population, but wanted the Senate based on a combined population and area formula. If Democrats got their way, the Upper Peninsula was in deep trouble. Butler knew she had to concede two House seats, but she was not about to give more. Delegates laughed when she explained why she was only willing to concede two House seats.

When I came down here, I came down dedicated to the proposition of having 7 from the upper peninsula. But since all this study has been made, I feel that I have to go along with the committee and give those 2 representatives to Wayne and Macomb. . . . But 4, I might as well go to Siberia. I would get a warmer reception there than I would in the upper peninsula if I went back with that. Even giving those 2 away, I felt a little like the woman in a court case where justice was meted out which was at least questionable, and she said: "There ain't no justice in this here land. I just got a divorce from my old man. I sure did laugh at the judge's decision. He gave him the children and the children weren't his'n."[3]

Civil Rights Commission

After a delay of nearly a week, discussions on a state civil rights commission resumed on Thursday, April 5. Five Republicans, including Alvin Bentley, John Hannah and John Martin, offered a substitute amendment to the Austin amendment. The substitute deleted the areas of discrimination specified in the Austin amendment: employment, education, housing and public accommodations. Richard Austin and Elliott filed an amendment to the substitute to add them back in. When a delegate stated that the four areas were made clear in the declaration of rights report on Committee Proposal 26—which included the new equal protection/nondiscrimination clause—and that it would be redundant to include them in the substitute amendment, Hatcher was quick to respond, explaining that he was referring to the declaration of rights committee report and that the committee never agreed to spell out the four areas of discrimination in Committee Proposal 26. The committee only agreed to insert language in the comment section of the new constitution that civil rights would include those four areas. The delegate responded, "Mrs. Hatcher is entirely correct, of course."[4]

Elliott then gave what would be her longest speech on the convention floor. She reminded delegates how wonderful it was when both parties communicated and cooperated in a spirit of true bipartisanship when the commission was first debated a week earlier. Regarding arguments that it was not necessary to spell out the four areas of discrimination, Elliott questioned opposition to include the four enumerated areas if the intent behind Committee Proposal 26 included employment, education, housing and public accommodations. Elliott then expressed her surprise that Hannah would join a revision after his previous support for a strong civil rights commission that contained the four areas:

> Some of the delegates have said to me, what does the negro, as one minority, want? Why are they pushing so hard for these rights? We are going to give them to them but it takes a little time for these things. I guess, Mr. President, you would have to be in the position of a negro to understand what is in their hearts and souls. To ask for the rights accorded to one under our constitution is not pushing. To want equal opportunities is not being impatient. To want to be free is not wanting to impose upon a society that has been closed to you.

Elliott drew an analogy between Black Americans and the children of Israel in their exodus from Egypt to the promised land. As their leader Joseph lay dying, he requested that once they reached the promised land they return to dig up his bones because "free bones would never rest easy in a slave grave." Elliott told delegates that this was how most Negros felt, that once their descendants reached the promised land—when Negros would live better lives and be truly free—they should "come back and dig up our bones, for free bones will never rest easy in a slave grave."[5] Although Elliott's speech was met with loud applause, the Austin/Elliott amendment was defeated 73 to 44, largely along party lines.

Various amendments were made to delete or weaken the Donnelly Amendment. Ann Donnelly strongly objected: "Do you want the courts to have jurisdiction in this matter or don't you?" She reminded them that she put her original amendment in on March 28 to provide an immediate and direct legal or equitable remedy in court. Donnelly felt *both* parties should have the right to go directly to court, even if the complaining party started the action in the civil rights commission. Delegates ultimately voted to adopt the Bentley/Hannah/Martin substitute to the Austin amendment 101 to 9. In the written explanation of his vote, Austin expressed his concerns that the major fields of discrimination were not spelled out in the substitute but that he had voted yes in the spirit of compromise: "We have retreated from the position we had arrived at on Thursday, March 29, when the amendment proposed by myself and a few other delegates was adopted by the committee of the whole."[6] In explaining her yes vote, Elliott acknowledged that the substitute was still a giant step forward in the area of civil rights because the legislature had failed to act.

After considering amendments to other sections of Committee Proposal 71, the proposal was adopted, as amended, and referred to style and drafting. Committee Proposal 71 now included a new section "i" which created a civil rights commission. On April 24, delegates voted to make Committee Proposal (i) a separate proposal known as Committee Proposal 71A.[7]

Committee proposal 71A was read a second time on April 24. Executive branch committee chairman Martin recommended that the proposal be adopted because it was almost exactly the proposal which had been adopted in committee of the whole. The one or two changes made by style and drafting, Martin told delegates, were not changes in substance. Seven amendments were offered, including amendments to eliminate or modify the Donnelly amendment. An exasperated Donnelly was the first to defend the last sentence. After more emotional debate, Committee Proposal 71A—a proposal to create a state civil rights commission—passed 110 to 9 with Donnelly's last sentence intact.[8]

Rule 9

Although the declaration of rights committee had voted on January 18 not to approve the *delegate* proposal that would allow owners of real property to sell to whomever they chose (Delegate Proposal 1007), the proposal was resurrected as a *committee* proposal (Committee Proposal 45). Committee Proposal 45 was introduced to the convention on April 10, 1962, and read: "The right of the owner of real property to convey, grant, or devise said property shall be limited only by general law. The Legislature shall not delegate this power."[9]

In what was perhaps her longest and most eloquent dissent on the convention floor, Hatcher warned delegates that the proposal would constitutionalize bigotry and discrimination and would set Michigan back one hundred years in the field of civil rights:

> Committee Proposal 45 is a transparent attempt to deprive negroes and others of the right to purchase, lease and hold real property by preventing the state from exercising its police power in such a way as to prevent prejudicial discrimination by would be sellers.[10]

The architect of the proposal dismissed Hatcher's arguments as mostly "irrelevant." Coleman Young quickly came to Hatcher's defense and reiterated the points she had made. Committee Proposal 45 was defeated three times. Rule 9—a proposed ruling—never went into effect.[11]

Changing Attitudes

Marjorie McGowan believed that changing attitudes—more so than courts, politics, marches or demonstrations—would break down the barriers to tolerance and friendship between different races.[12] Elliott also recognized the importance of changing attitudes as well as laws. Many of Con-Con's white delegation had had little or no interaction with people of color prior to the convention. Black delegates likely understood that they needed to be ambassadors as well as activists and that everything they said or did would be watched and judged.

Con-Con did change attitudes. Butler told delegates that Con-Con was her first experience knowing Negroes and that it had been a very wonderful experience for her: "I have deep respect for every person in this room and deep affection for those I have been closely associated with."[13] And it appears that at least one of the Black delegates felt similarly about Butler. He offered to travel to the U.P. to campaign for her when she ran for the state legislature after Con-Con ended. (Butler won the primary, but lost the general election.)

Happy Birthday Adelaide Hart

Birthdays were routinely acknowledged on the convention floor. Very few delegates or officers had poems written about them, however. Adelaide Hart had two—by a Democrat and a Republican.[14] Labor and convention leader William Marshall read the Democrats' tribute:

A is for Adelaide,
The Great crusader,
More crusades she enters
Than a gladiator.

D is for den mother
From dawn to dusk
Carrying the ball
For the rest of us.

E is for earnest,
The importance of being,
Which Adelaide shows
While others are fleeing.

L is for lioness,
Fierce in her den.
If they don't come to caucus
She'll swallow her men.

A if for affluence,
A schoolteacher's lot,
Earmark for highways
But for Adelaide not.

I is for irksome,
That Hale Brake is,
The more he 'coverts'
The confuser she is.

D is for don't,
Don't e'er vote your conscience,
Vote just for 'the package'
And all of that nonsense.

E is for energy,
Stores and potential,
And when it's all gone
What's the differential?

She don't have the votes!
Happy birthday, Miss Hart!

After the reading, Hart received a standing ovation.

Republican delegate and convention bard Herbert Turner poeticized Hart's hard work and leadership in a second birthday tribute:

I am not going to tell you how or when this came about
Because she's not historical, of that there is no doubt.
When a lady makes the experience age of 28 or 9
It's birthdays not of record, and this I think is fine.
This lady that I speak of is not afraid of work.
She digs into the problem whenever it may lurk.
With many years at teaching school she proved to be a master.
She even took a reading course to get the meaning faster.

And now in the convention, she's the leader of the crew.
She gets them in a huddle and suggests what they should do.
She had a brood of 44 but since then it made a gain
Of 2 more members strong and true aboard the Demo train.
She has proved herself a worker and leader from the start.
So now I would like to say to her: happy birthday Adelaide Hart.

The beloved Democratic caucus chair was obviously well liked and respected by many Republicans. The spirit of bipartisanship soon passed, however, when the convention returned to business.

Earmarking

Katherine Cushman told delegates that there was nothing ordained of heaven about gas and weight earmarking.[15] In what may have been her most unpopular stand, Cushman fought to eliminate earmarking from the constitution. Even leaguers Vera Andrus and Dorothy Judd failed to join Cushman in promoting the League of Women Voters long-established view that earmarking was not the way to meet Michigan's financial needs. Cushman agreed with the league that earmarking restricted the legislature and the governor in budgeting to meet the state's needs, that it didn't work in the long run and that earmarking led to more earmarking. Cushman specifically objected to continuing the earmarking of gasoline and motor vehicle taxes for highway purposes. The constitutional provision adopted by voters in 1938 reserved motor vehicle fuel and weight taxes exclusively for highways. Cushman had studied one aspect or another of state taxation as a member of the League of Women Voters, and her sixteen years of study had convinced her that earmarking did not work in the long run. She blamed earmarking for contributing to the state's 1959 financial crisis and warned that the state could face a $100 million debt by the end of the fiscal year. Cushman's pleas to eliminate earmarking fell on deaf ears. Her amendment to eliminate the earmarking of gas and weight taxes was defeated 103 to 9.[16] McGowan was the only female delegate to vote with her.

When it became evident that the convention was going to retain earmarking for highways, Cushman urged delegates to accept it for schools and libraries: "If we accept it for roads and turn it down for schools, we are going to appear to put roads on a higher level than schools."[17] Although Cushman considered penal fines funding for public libraries a form of earmarking, she supported it after the convention agreed to earmark funds for roads, local governments and schools:

> I would hate to see us . . . appearing to go for earmarking for every single pressure group except libraries. It seems to me that this might leave us open to the charge that we took the earmarking off for the one group that was perhaps the most defenseless group, the one with the smallest lobby.[18]

Natural Resources

On April 12, Judd and Cushman appeared before the emerging problems committee and introduced a proposed amendment to the committee's proposal on natural resources (Committee Proposal 125). The committee adopted their amendment and introduced it to the convention on April 18 as a committee amendment. A spirited discussion ensued in committee of the whole. Although Judd tried to assure delegates that the amended language would not affect existing water, air or property rights, the amendment was not adopted. A new natural resources section was ultimately approved and appears in the 1963 Constitution . Although declaratory in nature, the new section recognizes public concern for the conservation of natural resources and calls upon the legislature to take appropriate action to guard the people's interest in water, air and other natural resources. In 1962, the United States was in the throes of a population explosion. Delegates understood that as the population increased, so did pollution. According to an air pollution expert who testified before the emerging problems committee, Michigan was the only state that did not have, nor was in the process of adopting, a statewide anti-pollution law.[19]

Ruth Butler Gets Her Digs In

Butler was never reluctant to point out sexist remarks or behavior by either party. When convention vice president J. Edward Hutchinson told delegates that he was fearful not to carry over the estates of married women article into the new constitution for fear of "arousing" the female delegates and the majority of female voters who might become alarmed and not approve the new constitution, Butler couldn't resist commenting:

> I was amazed to have Mr. Hutchinson recognize the women, as the Republican men don't usually do that—and it was not as women of equal brain power or anything else, but as potential voters. La-de-da, Mr. Hutchinson! (laughter)[20]

The I Ain't Runnin' for Nothin' Club

By mid-April, Anne Conklin laid to rest any speculation that she might pursue a political career after Con-Con. Conklin told delegates that she was a charter member of the I Ain't Runnin' for Nothin' club. "If anybody can survive 7½ months of this and still wants to run, they are hardy people and I say: amen; let them run."[21]

Mackinac Bridge Refinancing

Butler and the other U.P. delegates offered an amendment to a committee proposal that would authorize the legislature to borrow money for the refunding of Mackinac Bridge Authority bonds. Their amendment was amended and passed, thus creating a new section in the constitution that would allow the legislature, by a two-thirds vote of each House, to borrow money for refunding of bonds issued by the Mackinac Bridge Authority. Butler felt this new addition to the constitution was one of her principal contributions to the convention.[22]

County Home Rule

In the end, Judd and Cushman's efforts to give counties the right to establish their own form of government without action by the legislature were defeated. The new constitutional section allowing for county home rule limited the structural changes a charter commission could propose by legislative action.[23]

Voting Age

Andrus was among the minority who favored lowering the voting age from twenty-one to nineteen. Andrus likely had something to do with the petition submitted to declaration of rights committee chairman James Pollock that was signed by 450 students of Port Huron Junior College asking that the voting age be reduced to nineteen. Andrus told delegates that her lifelong work with, and exposure to, young people greatly influenced her position. Although she acknowledged that her college students were a "select group," she expressed her confidence in nineteen-year-olds in general to be responsible and informed voters. In a very personal statement, Andrus shared with delegates how it felt to be denied the right to vote at age nineteen because women had not yet won the right to vote. She couldn't understand why her brother could vote and she couldn't. In a moving summation she told delegates:

> The world today is changing so rapidly; our problems are so serious. These are the people who are going to have to make our laws; these are the ones who are going to have to live under them. I would like very much to have people of the future look at this convention and say, "That 1962 constitutional convention saw the problems of the future. They had confidence in their young people and they put responsibility on them." I am sure the young people will meet that responsibility.[24]

After nearly two hours of debate, delegates voted 78 to 37 not to adopt the minority report amendment to lower the voting age. Elliott,

Hart and Hatcher were the other women who voted to lower the age to nineteen. Conklin, Donnelly, Judd, Ella Koeze and McGowan voted against lowering the voting age. Judd objected to the thinking that nineteen-year-olds were mature enough to vote simply because they were old enough to get married:

> There was a time when young men believed that they should not marry until they could support their families. Today it doesn't seem to be considered necessary, and I think particularly in the case of coeds who marry while they are still in college and give up their college and go to work to support the boys, this shows a great lack of vision as to their future needs, and these facts are evidences of irresponsibility.[25]

Although the voting age remained at twenty-one, Andrus surely felt some satisfaction that she tried her best to get the voting age lowered.

God, Country and Political Party

Koeze's dedication to the Republican party was obvious. As a longtime party organizer, Koeze preached the importance and advantage of party affiliation. To her, the two-party system was sacrosanct and independent voters were a threat to that system. She strongly believed that everyone should have to choose a political party that most closely reflected their ideals and aims. As she told delegates, "People should be proud of their faith, their country and above all, their party."[26]

Koeze felt that choosing a party was a responsibility:

> In this day and age, when we have a group of youngsters growing up that are independents, but who think there is some aura about being an independent, I think we should point up all the more to them that it is their responsibility to pick one of 2 of the major parties.[27]

Koeze wanted party preference to be made a matter of public record for Americans to pick a party and be proud of the party they pick.

Conklin also felt that everyone should identify their party affiliation. Conklin scoffed at the idea that future Con-Con candidates should run on a nonpartisan basis: "I do not believe that there is any such thing as a nonpartisan. Everybody believes in something." Conklin told delegates that she was "sick, sick, sick . . . of the idea that the nonpartisans are something better than those of us who believe in something." Conklin felt that election workers should identify their party affiliation: "I would feel a lot more comfortable if, when I went in to vote, I knew that there were 6 people sitting there, 3 of whom were watching the other 3."[28]

Michigan has had an open primary election since 1937, whereby voters can select their party ballot in secrecy. In a closed party primary, a person is required to register *with* a political party in order to vote in that party's primary. Closed primaries help political parties determine party affiliation. Conklin told delegates that both political parties spent a lot of time and money trying to identify party members, with the results of such efforts often being inconclusive and incorrect. She felt that a closed primary would strengthen and improve both political parties. To that end, Conklin joined thirty-six other delegates to cosponsor a bipartisan amendment to create a closed primary, the implementation of which would be handled by the legislature. Amendment sponsors were concerned about primary raiding, which occurred when members of the opposition party raided a party primary by voting for the weakest opposition candidate in the hopes that a weaker opposition candidate would be on the general election ballot. Political scientist Pollock told delegates that primary raiding was very rare. He cautioned delegates to remember that Michigan adopted the open primary because only the open primary preserved the secrecy of party choice. The open primary protected a person's privacy without fear of potential adverse social or economic consequences.

Proponents of the closed party primary felt that the reasons for open party primaries no longer existed. While they acknowledged that some employees had suffered adverse consequences for their votes in years past, they felt that those days were basically over. Hart may have made the strongest argument against closed primaries. Although she agreed that closed primaries made precinct work easier, she also felt they deterred many people from voting and registering their party affiliation. Hart concluded that it was far more important for everyone to register and vote than to assist political parties in identifying members. Young, one of the amendment cosponsors, reversed positions and urged delegates to vote against the amendment after Hart spoke. The amendment to create a close primary was defeated 60 to 55.

Some delegates felt that a person's politics should be their own private business unless they wanted it to be known. Other delegates, like Pollock, felt that neither a closed nor open primary should be constitutionalized.

Ella Koeze Continues to Speak Up

Koeze spoke up when she was not recognized on the convention floor:

> We got a little bit fouled up on this this morning, and I want to set the record straight. Mr. Hoxie got up to yield to Delegate Powell . . . and then he asked Mr. Habermehl to give the legal connotation of this particular proposal. Then I had prepared something of the history, but in the meantime Delegate Lesinski got up . . . and then of course this happened. I wasn't recognized . . . so Mr. Lesinski . . . offered his minority report amendment, and by that time I was lost in the fog.
>
> Then . . . there were a great many people ready to be recognized on debate, and we had gone on and on, and in the interest of time I was asked if I could perhaps reduce mine, and I felt it necessary to do that, but in the meantime I got a little bit angry because of the fact that I had spent some time on that. And here I am. I got up and made a silly little report to you which didn't amount to a hill of beans.[29]

She spoke up again when a legislative powers committee member failed to acknowledge her. He told delegates that the committee proposal being considered by the convention had "received 14 votes out of our 15-man committee, and I think the other man was absent at the time we passed it." Koeze, the only woman on the committee, corrected him. "Mr. Chairman, a correction please. I was on the committee. Mr. Wood said '14 men.'" Delegates laughed. A male delegate quipped: "What a gal she would have been back in the women's suffrage days."[30]

Proposal to Delete "Sex"

When Cushman's announcement was read by Secretary Chase on April 23 that women delegates, research consultants and others interested in "sex" in the new equal protection clause would meet the next morning, male delegates laughed.[31] Butler wondered what was going on. The equal protection/nondiscrimination clause had been unanimously passed on February 2. What was there to discuss?

Hatcher must have gotten an uneasy feeling in her gut when she heard about Cushman's announcement—the kind of feeling she used to get working in the UAW Women's Bureau pulling contracts that carried discriminatory clauses against women, such as unequal pay, marital status and female classifications. Although protective legislation for women had theoretically been designed to protect the health and safety of women workers, Hatcher knew that female classifications could limit the number and type of jobs and the type of pay for women. Hatcher had taken part in the UAW Women's Department attack on Michigan's protective labor legislation in an effort to combat sex discrimination in the workplace.[32] Some shops didn't want to hire married women, especially if their husbands worked in the same plant. She spent a lot of time in the late 1940s holding educational programs concerning enforcement of married women's job rights and kept a running list of locals that changed their bylaws to conform to the UAW's nondiscrimination policy. By the 1950s, discriminatory clauses against married women had virtually been eliminated in UAW contracts.[33]

On April 26, Cushman, Judd, McGowan and William Hanna offered an amendment—referred to as the Cushman amendment—to strike "sex" from the clause. Judd offered a second amendment, conditioned upon the adoption of the first, that would add the sentence "No woman shall be discriminated against because of sex or marital status in the securing of employment or in promotion therein."[34]

When Cushman rose to explain her amendment, some male delegates also rose, and the room erupted in laughter. Presiding chair Hutchinson, perhaps in an effort to mitigate the situation, described the standing ovation as a show of respect. Any chivalry was soon undermined when a male delegate quipped, "In case there is any doubt over what this was for, it was in honor of 'sex.' (laughter)." When Cushman stated her disappointment that delegates could not discuss the subject with a minimum of joking, she was met with more laughter. She was forced to ask delegates to pay attention. Whether prudish or immature, some male delegates were obviously uncomfortable discussing the word sex. One male delegate explained, "I guess the word 'sex' conjures up some sort of an embarrassment or something of the kind that causes people to take lightly its discussion." Another male delegate felt the word was undignified. He reasoned that it was not necessary to specify "sex" because the language of the clause "implied" that women were protected.[35] Years later, George Romney purportedly remarked that he could have supported the Equal Rights Amendment if it had just said "gender" instead of "sex."[36]

Hutchinson intervened again and instructed the men to "give the lady your respect and attention."[37] The convention then settled down and Cushman continued. Reading from the research statement of Dr. Alfred Kelly—a Con-Con codirector of research and drafting—and a memo prepared by research staff, Cushman posited that including "sex" in the equal protection clause could make reasonable classification on the basis of sex impossible. In that event, Cushman warned, the legislature would be unable to enact protective legislation for women, such as working hours and conditions.

When Judd stood to speak on her amendment, some male delegates gestured in prayer. Judd responded, "Mr. President and gentlemen, I'm not quite sure what that moment of silent prayer was about but I hope you were praying for endurance to listen to our problems."[38] Judd warned that including "sex" in the clause could deprive women of some of the special privileges they currently enjoyed, such as alimony and special working conditions. Judd pointed out that her amendment addressed discrimination on account of marital status as well as sex because women were the first to be let go in times of unemployment. Judd believed her amendment would combat the type of discrimination that was most difficult for women at the time. Unlike Cushman and Judd, McGowan never explained on the record why she felt that the word "sex" should be removed from the clause.

Law professor and declaration of rights second vice chairman Harold Norris was the first to object to the amendment. Donnelly was the second. Donnelly told delegates that Cushman, Judd and McGowan were ill-advised on the law and that the amendment she was going to offer would put their fears to rest. Donnelly's amendment would add the sentence "This shall not be construed to prevent reasonable classification for the protection of women" to the equal protection clause.[39] It was not adopted.

Dr. Pollock urged delegates to retain the word "sex" and reminded them that his committee had put the word in with "care and caution" and "for good and sufficient reason." The Cushman amendment was defeated 69 to 44. Because delegates had voted to divide the Cushman and Judd amendments and vote on them separately, Judd withdrew her amendment after the Cushman amendment was defeated.[40] Judd told delegates that the two amendments should never have been divided because one was only useful if the other was adopted.

Committee Proposal 26 was again passed 118 to 0, but Butler, Hatcher and Donnelly were still concerned. Less than three months prior, the convention had unanimously adopted Committee Proposal 26 with sex included as a protected class. Now, forty-four delegates were willing to remove the word. The women were right to be concerned. The next day, attorney-delegate Robert Danhof sought a reconsideration of the vote on the Cushman amendment. Danhof argued that because the subject was treated with levity, delegates didn't consider the matter or the repercussions of leaving the word in. Echoing Danhof's claim that delegates had not seriously considered the matter, another delegate stated that there was a tendency "on the part of some of us . . . to look slightly askance at something that is promoted by the fair ladies all by themselves."[41] (He apparently forgot that William Hanna also cosponsored the amendment.)

Hatcher rose first to oppose Danhof's motion to reconsider the vote. She denied that the amendment had not been considered seriously or thoroughly. Pointing to her considerable experience working in the field of labor problems as they affected female workers, Hatcher said the declaration of rights committee had well founded reasons to place "sex" in the equal protection clause. Hatcher cited a Utah Supreme Court case which upheld constitutional language almost identical to the wording in Committee Proposal 26. After refuting legal arguments pertaining to Danhof's motion to reconsider, Hatcher set forth practical ones. With twenty-five to thirty more proposals for the convention to take up, Hatcher complained that the motion was taking up unnecessary time. With approximately eleven session days left, Hatcher told delegates that they would be working until 1972 if they started reconsidering every single proposal.

Donnelly accused certain male delegates of attempting to becloud the issue, pointing out that the matter had been debated and voted upon more than once. She charged that if these men were really concerned, they would have voted for her amendment. Despite Donnelly and Hatcher's protests, Danhof's motion to reconsider was adopted 64 to 60. An angry Butler told delegates that the women were quite sure that they were going to have a great deal of opposition. A rights committee member validated Butler's statement when he told delegates that "these people were warned time and time again during the committee that they were only looking for trouble."[42] "These people" no doubt were Butler and Hatcher.

As she had done throughout the convention, Butler continued to point out how male and female delegates had been treated differently and that two of the most important committees, legislative organization and finance and taxation, still had no woman on them. Butler also pointed out that no woman was appointed to the committee to meet with the legislature, to be on a special committee to speed things up or to preside in committee of the whole.

Although Conklin favored striking "sex" from the clause, she admonished the men for their immature behavior: "I think that yesterday there was a lot of hilarity on the subject, and I don't think that we have straightened up too much more this morning."[43] When the Cushman amendment failed in a tie vote—59 to 59—Conklin unsuccessfully attempted to get the Chair to break the tie.

Donnelly then made a motion to have her amendment to ensure reasonable classification for the protection of women reconsidered. Her motion to reconsider passed and her amendment to add the sentence

"This shall not be construed to prevent reasonable classification for the protection of women" was adopted. Committee Proposal 26, as amended, was adopted 116 to 3 and referred back to style and drafting.[44] "Sex" had dodged the bullet again.

Exhausted

While announcing requests for leave at the beginning of the April 30th session, convention secretary Chase announced that one of the delegates had been hospitalized for exhaustion.[45]

.

IX.

May 1962

ay had finally arrived and it seemed inconceivable that the convention could complete its work by May 15. A collective angst hung over Constitution Hall. Partisan bickering had intensified since George Romney announced his candidacy for governor on February 10. So did the anger and resentment at Con-Con's fifty-seven lawyers.

Lock Up All the Lawyers

Assigning twenty lawyers to the twenty-one-member committee on the judiciary was a bad idea according to James Pollock. It wasn't so great for the nonlawyer committee member either. Initially, delegates joked that pharmacist Sidney Barthwell was there to provide aspirin for the rest of the committee. A more likely story is that Barthwell was the one who needed aspirin. Fed up with the lawyers' excessive haggling, Barthwell walked into a committee meeting one day with the largest jar of aspirin that committee chairman Robert Danhoff had ever seen. Barthwell plunked the jar down in front of members and said, "I'm tired of getting headaches from all you lawyers."[1] Even Marjorie McGowan admitted that searching for judicial truth with twenty lawyers became laborious at times.[2]

Judicial committee headaches became convention headaches once judicial committee proposals were reported out to committee of the whole. Pollock said that the excessive debating by the lawyers gave the rest of Con-Con "hiccups" for about three weeks. Delegates were frustrated when lawyers discussed relatively unimportant matters that only interested them.[3] Many delegates felt like leaving the floor at times and letting the lawyers work things out. However, when they did, the lawyers still could not agree. And while lawyers weren't the only delegates guilty of excessive oratory, it certainly seemed so to many nonlawyer delegates. After one very long day of debate, Ella Koeze proposed that delegates lock up all the lawyers until they could decide what they wanted. And if they couldn't decide, she proposed that all of the lawyers be locked out of the convention until the laypeople could decide. Delegates laughed and applauded.[4]

Convention leaders became increasingly critical of the long-winded debates. Delegates started walking out and missing crucial votes, causing them to reverse their votes the next day. Soon substantial numbers of delegates left the floor during debate and only returned to cast their votes. Melvin Nord's resolution to bar unexcused delegates who left the convention didn't seem to help much. Things got so bad, Anne Conklin made the following statement before discussing a committee proposal: "I would like to point out to the laymen, if there are any left in the room."[5]

Donnelly felt the sting of lawyer backlash as vice chairman of the subcommittee on eminent domain, which addressed the taking of private property for public use. Donnelly's subcommittee wanted to change how the highway department acquired land for its highway right-of-way. The subcommittee wanted the state to first pay property owners before taking their land. Pursuant to highway practices, hearings on the necessity of taking private property were held first. Damages, or payment to the property owner, were determined at a second hearing. In defending the subcommittee's paid-first provision, Donnelly argued that many property owners did not receive compensation until months, sometimes years, after the necessity hearing when the property might be devalued. "Do you want the property taken, used and removed from the control of . . . the owner . . . and have . . . a jury two or three years later try to determine what that property looked like when the highway is rolling over it?"[6] The subcommittee also considered making all condemnation hearings a matter for circuit court. Article XIII, Section 2 of the 1908 constitution provided that such hearings could be held before a "jury of twelve freeholders" or "not less than three commissioners." A newspaper article predicted outcries from the highway department.[7]

The committee proposal on eminent domain was introduced to the convention on April 18. It incorporated the subcommittee recommendation that property owners be compensated first before their property was seized. Proposal opponents were concerned about highway construction delays and increased right-of-way costs. Donnelly and other subcommittee members were concerned with protecting the rights of individual property owners.[8] By May 1 some subcommittee members expressed their frustrations about how the committee proposal was handled during committee of the whole debates. J. Don Lawrence complained that it was either addressed late at night or voted upon with insufficient delegates present. Donnelly complained about the unexcused absences—something Nord had attempted to address weeks earlier with his resolution. "This is not fair," Donnelly protested. "It is not the way to write a constitution."[9]

Debates were heated inside and outside Constitution Hall. Subcommittee chairman Paul Mahinske told delegates that he, Donnelly and "the loyal opposition" almost got evicted from the Capitol Park Motor Hotel during dinner after they got into a "violent argument." Whatever was happening on or off the convention floor, Donnelly felt moved to tell delegates that her subcommittee had been "unusually abused." She also sounded off against those who felt that the subcommittee proposals were self-serving and created to generate more work for attorneys. Donnelly was clearly upset that people lacked confidence in her subcommittee members and questioned their integrity as lawyers and as delegates: "Apparently, as this convention has rolled forward, the attorneys have gone from bad to worse."[10]

In the end, the eminent domain section that was ultimately approved contained two simple statements: "Private property shall not be taken

for public use without just compensation therefor being first made or secured in a manner prescribed by law. *Compensation shall be determined in a court of record.*"[11] But the aspersions that had been leveled against Donnelly's subcommittee—and the legal profession—were hurtful, especially to such proud attorneys as Donnelly.

Looking at the Total Document

For Katherine Cushman and the other style and drafting committee members, the first week of May was grueling. They had less than a week to review all of the committee proposals in order. Downstairs in Committee Room G, the heap of green paper proposals looked like a "green mountain."[12] Cushman was used to putting together publications for the League of Women Voters. She edited and authored the 150-page League of Women Voters book, *Dearborn and Its Government.*[13] But that effort was no comparison to what would be required of her to help assemble the proposed new state constitution. The first week of May would be the first time that the committee would be able to view the entire document. Cushman and the other committee members were under tremendous pressure to finish their work by May 7 when the convention reconvened.

The Fight to Retain "Sex"

There was still so much work to do before delegate salaries ended on May 15. On May 7, William Cudlip, on behalf of the style and drafting committee, made motions to reconsider the Cushman amendment and Ann Donnelly's last sentence "This shall not be construed to prevent reasonable classification for the protection of women." Cudlip resurrected prior arguments that the amendment had not been seriously considered and gave undue weight to the lawyers who favored deleting the word. Cudlip relied heavily on the Con-Con research paper written by University of Michigan constitutional law professor Dr. Paul Kauper. Lillian Hatcher pointed out that Kauper's opinion was a male opinion and he would not have the same viewpoint that a woman would have.

She denied claiming exclusive rights to fighting the battle of the sexes but reminded delegates that the men and women on the declaration of rights committee saw fit to include "sex" in the equal protection clause. As for the deference given to attorney-delegates, delegates laughed when Hatcher said, "I believe that the 57 attorneys here haven't agreed on any one particular thing up to this time. And I don't see any reason why there should be any unanimity of opinion at this particular time."[14]

Style and drafting committee member Harold Norris chastised the committee for offering a motion to reconsider in the absence of some committee members. Emotions intensified and Norris had to ask the chair to maintain order so that he could be heard: "I trust . . . that some dignity and status might be accorded to the speaker."[15]

Donnelly couldn't believe that the Cushman amendment was being considered for a third time. Cushman told delegates that she believed every delegate wanted women protected but contended that discriminations against women were better dealt with by specific statutes than a constitutional statement that might do away with current protections that women needed. When Cudlip told delegates that women needed to be discriminated against for their own good, Donnelly fired back:

This attitude has existed for, certainly, more years than I have lived. I don't want it to continue to exist. I am very, very, very mindful of the discrimination against women. I have found no discrimination for my protection. . . . I think the underlying motive behind this is not to protect women. And I object to these amendments very strenuously. I don't think they will protect women. I think they aid in discrimination against them.[16]

The clamor inside Constitution Hall became so great that Hart asked delegates to go out in the corridor if they wanted to caucus "so those of us who would like to hear the debate may be privileged to do so."[17] Republican attorney J. Don Lawrence made a last plea to keep "sex" in the clause:

If this is so wrong, then those of you who feel it is a sword instead of a shield had better take out "race, color, religion and national origin" because it will harm those who seek to be protected on those grounds as well.[18]

Minutes later, the amendments to remove "sex" from the equal protection clause and Donnelly's last sentence were adopted 82 to 48. The vote was largely along party lines. Conklin voted with Cushman, Judd and McGowan to remove the word. Republicans Vera Andrus, Ruth Butler, Donnelly and Koeze joined Democrats Hart, Daisy Elliott and Hatcher to retain the word.

In a letter to the Michigan chapter of the American Association of University Women, Judd explained why she and Cushman were concerned to carry out the desire of the League of Women Voters of Michigan to secure a provision guaranteeing to women freedom from discrimination on account of sex or marital status for securing a job. Judd recounted how male delegates didn't take the matter seriously until Third Reading when "some of the lawyers woke up" after consulting with two Con-Con research staff members, University of Michigan law professor Charles Joiner and Wayne State University history professor Alfred Kelley and reading the opinion of U of M constitutional law professor Kauper. Judd wrote, "It was, by this time, however, too late to do anything about the one point of nondiscrimination with regard to securing a job."[19] Judd's letter further indicates that the American Civil Liberties Union of Michigan sent a memorandum to the delegates explaining the adverse effect of keeping the word "sex" in the nondiscrimination clause.

As of 2025, "sex" is still not included in the equal protection/ nondiscrimination clause of Michigan's constitution.

Estates of Married Women

The estates of married women section in the 1908 constitution was one area where female delegates agreed that protections for women were needed. Article XVI, Section 8 provided:

> The real and personal estate of every woman, acquired before marriage, and all property to which she may afterwards become entitled by gift, grant, inheritance or devise shall be and remain the estate and property of such woman, and shall not be liable for the debts, obligations or engagements of her husband, and may be devised or bequeathed by her as if she were unmarried.

When the section was first debated in committee of the whole on April 13, one male delegate argued that when the article was originally enacted in 1850, women needed protections, but did not need such protections in 1962. Koeze asked him what made him think that things had changed since 1850: "You talk about . . . a partnership; sure, but that partnership is usually 80–20."[20] Donnelly told delegates that to say that married women did not need protection was to ignore the facts of life. Donnelly, who likely understood dower rights better than most delegates, told delegates that the issue was not as simple as the men were "laughingly" twisting it.

On May 8, several male delegates offered an amendment that rewrote the section to also favor men:

> The real and personal estate of every *man and* woman, acquired before marriage, and all property to which *each* may afterwards become entitled by gift, grant, inheritance or devise, shall be and remain the estate and property of *each*, and shall not be liable for the debts, obligations or engagements of *each other*, and may be devised or bequeathed by *each* as if *each* were unmarried.[21]

On its face, the 1908 section appears to discriminate against men and the May 8 proposed section appears equitable. In reality, women still needed dower protections in 1962, given the gross economic disparity between most men and women at that time. Thus, female delegates were not amused by the men's amendment. Butler, Donnelly and Hatcher— the three women who had fought so hard to keep "sex" in the equal protection clause—were not amused. Butler came out swinging:

> Women have been treated this afternoon as they have been treated each time we have asked something that sex was referred to or that women's rights were referred to, and I think that the facetiousness is very indicative of the way that the men in this constitutional convention feel about anything that we are trying to advance for women.[22]

Hatcher's years of fighting for women's rights culminated in one of her best speeches on the convention floor:

We have talked about the questions of the rights of women and we lost a very important battle yesterday when we removed it from the equal protection section.

I think . . . that if we wanted to be very critical and analytical about some of the things that are happening right here in this convention, we could point out that we have violated the state labor laws affecting women constantly throughout the length and breadth of this convention, because women have worked more than 9 hours a day and more than 10 hours a day, and I believe the state statute speaks out and is opposed to women working those hours. So we have not reduced ourselves to this childish prank and jest and so on.

It is true that a lot of women should be at home as one of the brothers back here just said, but a lot of them don't have homes to go to—not unless they are working—and the intent and purpose that was behind "sex" being included was not for women who have great inheritance to share or stocks to share and so on. It was for women who work for a living and those who work for a livelihood, and I think that that would be the sense and the seriousness of the inclusion of the word "sex" in the equal protection section that we voted against yesterday.[23]

Before the vote was taken, Donnelly demanded the yeas and nays. The amendment was defeated 97 to 13. Koeze told delegates that she was glad that she was not married to any of the thirteen male delegates who voted for the amendment.[24] A substitute offered by Butler which retained the original 1908 estates of married women section and added clarifying language was adopted and appears in the 1963 constitution as Article X, Section 1.

Let's Agree to Disagree

Partisan animosity had become such a problem that Hart felt the need to speak out. There was still so much work to do and wasting time bickering made no sense to her. She chastised delegates to stop their innuendos and get on with the business of the convention. Not wanting to further inflame an already volatile atmosphere, Hart added, "Let's at least be friends while we disagree."[25]

Adelaide Hart's Saddest Moment

After working tirelessly for nearly seven and a half months, voting against the proposed new education article weighed heavily on Hart:

> I think that the saddest moment I have known in this convention was at the time of second reading when I had to urge my fellow Democrats to vote no on the educational proposal. Many good things are contained in this article, many things that I would wish for the educational system of Michigan. However, I believe that the things that are not good outweigh those that are good.[26]

Committee chairman Alvin Bentley expressed his sadness that his "good friend and able vice chairman" could not support the article. Many years later, Hart would still recall her time on the education committee as being very discouraging.[27]

The issue of whether or not to elect or appoint the Superintendent of Public Instruction was probably the most controversial issue faced by the education committee. The state superintendent had been an elective officer for more than a century.[28] Under the new education article, the superintendent would be appointed by an eight-member State Board of Education. Hart felt strongly that the change demoted the state superintendent and that it eliminated his position as an independent leader who derived his power from the people via the electoral process.

Con-Con Pays Homage

Delegates started the morning of May 9 with an attitude of gratitude. They adopted resolutions thanking Lansing's mayor, city council and civic center board and staff. Constitutional convention staff were honored with a resolution and standing ovation. The Citizens Research Council of Michigan was also honored in a resolution for its objective and excellent research studies and publications. The publications had been used extensively by delegates and committees as reliable factual sources throughout all phases of the convention's work.[29] Ever the school teacher, Hart made a point of recognizing an "exemplary citizen" in the audience. The Jackson, Michigan, woman had been written about in the newspapers for taking the bus to Lansing—an approximate forty-mile distance—every day for weeks to observe the convention.[30] The remainder of the almost twelve-hour day was spent on Third Reading.

Last Day

Conklin was in a fine mood as she wondered which delegates had sent her a lovely corsage that morning. The card was signed "Republican mafia."[31] The popular delegate would miss her new friends, but she looked forward to the long break before the convention met again for the final wrap-up session on August 1. It was hard to imagine not coming to Constitution Hall again. Soon, the auditorium would be returned to its former state and Constitution Hall would exist no more. Still, there would be many wonderful memories to occupy her mind for years to come.

Butler was also in high spirits. The Michigan Federation of Business and Professional Women recently named her as the outstanding woman in a policy-making post in the state of Michigan.[32] The convention would soon end, and Butler felt good about Con-Con's accomplishments. She believed that she had helped produce a better constitution for her seven grandchildren and their descendants. Butler looked forward to returning home to family and friends and her beloved Copper Country.

Emotions were high as delegates gathered in Constitution Hall. It was nearly impossible not to get goose bumps when President Stephen Nisbet announced, "The president lays before the convention the complete document, the proposed constitution of the state of Michigan."[33]

There was a new constitution. There was finally an actual document to present to voters. Of course, delegates still needed to adopt the document, but that was a formality. Republicans had the votes.

Democrats didn't. Nisbet expressed his empathy: "The chair realizes this is a difficult day."[34]

Delegates spent the morning debating last-minute amendments and motions to reconsider. Shortly after lunch, thirty-four Democrats, including Hart, Elliott and Hatcher, offered a substitute to the proposed constitution. Recognizing that it might be her last statement from the convention floor, Elliott expressed her gratitude for the fellowship shown by delegates before briefly discussing a few of the proposed changes.[35]

Although the substitute had no chance of passage, some Republicans were openly critical. Koeze likened delegates who opposed the new constitution to spoiled children who refused to play if they didn't get their own way. Pollock expressed his sadness and disappointment that a "hastily assembled patchwork and objectionable substitute" had been offered for "our carefully deliberated document." Pollock called the substitute destructive of convention unity, partisan, self-serving and unworthy. Judd praised the proposed new constitution but stopped short of criticizing the substitute: "I think each one of us would have a lot of fun writing a constitution that would satisfy us individually 100 percent. But it might be a little confusing to the voters to have 144 different constitutions to choose from." Bentley praised the proposed new constitution and the hard work of every delegate: "I do not believe that ever in the history of this state have we ever had 144 more dedicated and more qualified citizens of Michigan assemble under one roof who have worked longer hours or more tirelessly." John Martin was similarly diplomatic in rejecting the substitute and referred to Democrats twice as "our friends." As expected, the substitute was defeated 100 to 43, almost entirely along party lines. Elliott, Hart and Hatcher voted for the substitute. Andrus, Butler, Conklin, Cushman, Donnelly, Judd, Koeze and McGowan voted against it.[36]

Expressing mixed emotions, Hatcher told delegates that she could not approve the proposed new constitution primarily because its search and seizure provision had been declared unconstitutional by several Michigan courts as an unlawful invasion of the right to privacy and because "sex" had been deleted from the equal protection clause. Hatcher felt that the deletion of the word offered a disservice to the many women wage earners of Michigan.

Cushman received applause when she stated that she would whole-heartedly support the new constitution. Although Cushman told delegates that she was unhappy that all of her views were not included in the new document, she still felt that the new constitution was a vast improvement over the old. Romney called for unity and pointed out that overall, the substitute made few changes to the new constitution. Echoing Cushman, Koeze stated that although the new constitution did not fulfill many of her hopes, it was still superior to the old constitution. After a few additional delegate comments were made, the convention approved the proposed new constitution 99 to 44, almost entirely along party lines. Elliott, Hart and Hatcher voted against it. Andrus, Butler, Conklin, Cushman, Donnelly, Judd, Koeze and McGowan voted for it.[37]

Democrats explained their no vote and reminded delegates that the new constitution could have been divided into controversial and noncontroversial parts.[38] (New York had successfully divided the vote on its new constitution.) Now, the proposed new constitution would be submitted to the voters as one document—a take-it-or-leave-it package.

Marjorie McGowan Rebuked

The next day, Coleman Young's article on Con-Con's Black delegation appeared in the *Michigan Chronicle*.[39] Young lauded the other Black delegates but made a blistering criticism of McGowan. Young told readers that McGowan had continually been on the opposite side of many issues supported by Black delegates and most Democrats. He also chastised her popularity with Republicans. Young told readers that McGowan was more responsible than any other delegate for the inclusion of provisions in the proposed new constitution which tended to give police a blank check to search citizens outside their homes.

Some Democratic party leaders also held a grudge against McGowan for voting her conscience throughout the convention. McGowan was not the only Democrat to cross party lines. Cushman often did. But McGowan seemed to have incurred the brunt of the Dems' anger. It was reported that some party officials tried to block her appointment by Attorney General

Robert F. Kennedy to the U.S. Justice Department, although they had originally sanctioned it.[40] Her federal appointment had been cleared before Con-Con ended, however, and McGowan would commence her duties as a trial attorney in the criminal division in June 1962.

X.

Last Day

Constitution Hall
Lansing Civic Center
August 1, 1962

Delegates looked much more rested and relaxed as they gathered in Constitution Hall for Con-Con's last session. Michigan State University carried the proceedings live on radio through WKAR-FM. The lack of carpeting and drapes made acoustics more difficult. President Stephen Nisbet cautioned one delegate to stand far enough back from the microphone so that his voice would carry better.[1]

Almost all of the delegates—including the eleven female delegates—were present. For all their bickering and fighting, delegates were still a family and they overwhelmingly favored having regular reunions after Con-Con ended.[2] Anne Conklin, Daisy Elliott and Ella Koeze were appointed to the sixteen-member reunion committee. Many friendships were strengthened during Con-Con, but many more were formed by the shared experience. Vera Andrus, Katherine Cushman and Dorothy Judd would remain lifelong friends. Working together on the League of Women Voters' Con-Con platform and their many Capitol Park Motor Hotel breakfast meetings had brought them closer together. The bonding experience of seven and a half months at Con-Con was not just felt by delegates. Staff had also worked tirelessly with delegates, and many Con-Con staffers were present for the final session. They had come without pay so that they could see the delegates one more time. Delegates were happy to see them.

The final passage of the constitution, as amended, was adopted 98 to 43, right before lunch. After lunch, Democrats sought to modify or replace the Preface and Address to the People. They felt that the documents should have been neutral in tone. Instead of just pointing out changes that had been made to the 1908 constitution, many editorializing statements were made that certain sections were "improved" or "strengthened." Democrats feared that the positive spin would aid Republicans in getting the proposed new constitution ratified. Adelaide Hart and Elliott cosponsored an amendment with eleven other Democrats to include the minority view to the Preface. They reasoned that voters should be presented with both the majority and minority points of view before voting on the proposed new constitution. The amendment was defeated, undoubtedly along party lines. One delegate motioned to replace the Address to the People with the Citizens Research Council of Michigan's publication *The Proposed Constitution—A Comparison with the Present Constitution*.[3] His amendment also failed.

A final budget was approved, including funding for 200,000 copies of the complete Address to the People, and 400,000 copies of the Preface to the address. The convention also adopted a resolution thanking the legislature for appropriating an additional $75,000 to wind up the affairs of the convention. At 3:10 p.m., the convention recessed until 5:00 p.m., at which time President Nisbet reported that an official copy of the revised constitution had been delivered to the secretary of state. Before the convention adjourned without day at 5:15 p.m., Nisbet thanked delegates and told them that he had never been associated with a finer or more dedicated or devoted group than them.[4]

Conclusion

A s Democrats had feared, George Romney was elected governor in November 1962. And as legislators had feared, many Con-Con delegates ran for the legislature after Con-Con ended. Daisy Elliott won her seat for state representative. The Democratic party mounted a vigorous campaign to oppose the new constitution and chose Adelaide Hart to lead the party's fight. While Hart acknowledged that there was much good in the new constitution, she felt the bad so outweighed the good that the constitution had to be defeated.[1]

Con-Con's proposed new constitution was narrowly approved by voters on April 1, 1963. A recount established the vote as 810,860 to 803,436.[2] Regardless of if one thought that the new constitution was inferior or superior to the 1908 constitution, everyone agreed that improvements had been made. The 1963 Constitution was shorter, better worded and better arranged than the 1908 constitution. The 1908 constitution had 21,790—and the 1963 constitution 19,203—words. Fifty-five outdated and irrelevant sections were eliminated. Seventy-three new sections were added.[3] Only sixteen sections of the 1908 constitution remained unchanged. Phraseology was improved and clarifications made to accord with judicial decisions. Style and drafting committee members like Katherine Cushman spent countless hours reviewing the constitution with a fine-tooth comb. The committee, aided by research staff, worked diligently to weed out ambiguities, inconsistencies, unclear language or possible omissions, as well as arrange the document in a logical, easy-to-read format.

Female delegates played significant roles in many of the positive changes made. This was particularly evident in the areas of civil and individual rights, education, local government and reorganization of the executive branch. The establishment of a civil rights commission in the new constitution was considered one of Con-Con's greatest achievements. Hart, Lillian Hatcher and Elliott in particular were behind the campaign to create the commission. Elliott and Hart were assigned to the subcommittee responsible for recommending whether or not a civil rights commission should be created in the constitution. The inclusion of an equal protection/nondiscrimination clause was another major advancement in the new constitution. The 1908 constitution lacked such a clause. The new equal protection clause protected against discrimination because of religion, race, color or national origin in the enjoyment of civil and political rights and granted equal protection of the laws to all persons. Although Con-Con made considerable gains in the area of civil rights, women's rights did not fare as well. Despite a strong and valiant fight by Ruth Butler, Ann Donnelly, Hatcher and several others, "sex" was removed as a protected class from the new clause.

Eminent domain subcommittee vice chairman Donnelly scored a victory for property owners by insisting that they be paid *before* their property was taken for public use. Property owners had previously been subjected to great abuse, especially when property was taken for highway purposes. The revised section also provided that compensation shall be determined in proceedings in a court of record, whereas the 1908 constitution provided that just compensation would be determined by a jury of not less than three commissioners appointed by a court of record.

Vera Andrus was largely responsible for getting a new section in the constitution establishing and providing financial support for public community and junior colleges. Community colleges did not exist in

1907, and Andrus helped delegates understand the growing importance of community colleges in Michigan's educational system.

As a member of the subcommittee on metropolitan areas and intergovernmental relations, Cushman was instrumental in getting a new section in the constitution on intergovernmental cooperation to encourage the solution of metropolitan problems. In 1961, America was in the throes of a Baby Boom, which required more governmental units and services. Cushman's expansive knowledge of local government made her realize that a strong metropolitan section was needed in the new constitution to address problems shared by other units of local government. She also understood that local governments needed to cooperate to provide services more efficiently and economically, address problems that transcended the boundaries of individual governmental units and avoid duplication of services. Cushman strongly influenced the revision of Article VIII, Section 31 in the 1908 constitution on metropolitan government—including broader and more flexible language—to allow the legislature to set up more efficient forms of metropolitan government.

Judd's fight for county home rule can be traced back to the 1930s. Although Judd and Cushman were unsuccessful in their efforts to give counties the right to establish their own form of government without legislative action, thanks to their efforts the new constitution allowed for county home rule, which was not available under the 1908 constitution.

Major revisions were made in the executive article. A regrouping of the state's 126-plus executive agencies into 20 departments was a significant improvement. Terms for governor, lieutenant governor, secretary of state and attorney general were increased from two to four years. The powers of the governor were also expanded. As members of the executive branch committee and subcommittee on executive reorganization, Elliott and Hart played important roles in the aforementioned changes.

Apportionment and state fiscal stabilization fueled the call for a convention, yet no female delegate was appointed to the legislative organization or finance and taxation committees that reviewed these issues in depth. The revised apportionment article changed the apportioning method and created a commission to periodically reapportion the House and Senate seats.[4] The redistricting method ran into trouble in 1964, when the U.S. Supreme Court held that a similar formula violated the Equal Protection Clause of the Fourteenth Amendment, and the commission was invalidated in 1982. In 2018 Michigan voters passed a constitutional amendment to create the Independent Citizens Redistricting Commission.[5]

Cushman's efforts to eliminate earmarking were unsuccessful. She blamed earmarking for contributing to the state's 1959 financial crisis and warned that the state could face a $100 million debt by the end of the fiscal year. Efforts to include a graduated income tax were also unsuccessful. However, a new section dealing with the borrowing power of the state was created to give the state greater flexibility to meet cash crises within the general fund by permitting short-term borrowing not exceeding 15 percent of the state's undedicated revenues during the previous fiscal year (approximately $70 million in 1962).[6] The 1908 constitution limited borrowing to an unrealistic $250,000. This new section was created to end the problem which caused Michigan's cash crisis in the late 1950s.[7] Without the input, advocacy and expertise of Con-Con's female delegates, particularly in the areas of civil rights, local government, education and executive branch reorganization and improvement, the new constitution would have been a lesser document.

Afterword

Vera

Monuments, even of stone, are temporary. But Vera Andrus built one of the most lasting kind in helping mold the minds of so many young people of this community in the ways of social understanding and constructive citizenship.

—"Vera Andrus Asked Much, Gave Much,"
Port Huron Times Herald, September 3, 1976

Vera Andrus did not seek political office after Con-Con ended. Instead, she returned to Port Huron and continued to involve herself in the League of Women Voters of Michigan and in civic affairs. She became a member of the Committee for Commission-Manager Government. The commission-manager form of local government had been one of her first league crusades in the early 1940s. In a thank-you letter from the general chairman of the committee, Andrus was commended for her interest in sound municipal government and for alerting Port Huron citizens "to the need for their interest and concern in maintaining a progressive form of local government."[1] Vera Andrus passed away in 1976 at the age of eighty.

Ruth

If anyone ever needed proof that senior citizens can make a major contribution to society even while struggling against ill health, Ruth Butler is proof.

—Governor William G. Milliken, "Ruth G. Butler, Active in Republican Party," *Detroit News*, March 31, 1981

Ruth Butler became one of the most politically active women in the history of the Upper Peninsula. After Con-Con, she made an unsuccessful bid for the Michigan House of Representatives in 1962. In 1966, she was the first woman elected to the Houghton Village Council, making her the first woman to be elected in the council's 114-year history.[2] She was also the first woman in the U.P. to serve in such a capacity in local government. Butler became so well known for her work on the Upper Peninsula State Fair Board that the exhibition building on the U.P. State Fair Grounds in Escanaba was named in her honor.[3] Governor Romney appointed Butler to the Commission for the Equality of Women. Governor William G. Milliken appointed her as a delegate to the White House Conference on Problems of the Aging. Milliken called her an inspiration to people of all ages.

Butler lived the rest of her life in her beloved Upper Peninsula. As she told an interviewer in 1972, "there's no place that you can go that's more beautiful than the Copper Country. Rain or shine, snow or winter sun, it is a beautiful section."[4] Butler died in Marquette in 1981 at the age of eighty-nine.[5]

Anne

The darling of the Constitutional Convention is petite Delegate Anne M. Conklin, 37, of Livonia, who admits she was nipped by the political bug when she was 11 and still has the virus.

—Ken McCormack, "'The Den Mother': Housewife-Politician Darling of Con-Con," *Detroit Free Press*, January 28, 1962

It does not appear that Anne Conklin ever held public office again. How she spent the remaining thirteen years of her life is unclear. Conklin died in 1975 at the age of fifty.

Perhaps the greatest takeaway from Conklin's service as a Con-Con delegate is that she became one in the first place. And at no small sacrifice. With the exception of Katherine Cushman who had a sixteen-year-old daughter at home, Conklin was the only female delegate to have school-aged children at home. Her children were ten, fourteen and seventeen when Con-Con began. Conklin relied on her seventeen-year-old daughter to assume many of the homemaking responsibilities in her absence.

Any lawmaking body should be diverse, and Conklin brought the average citizen's perspective to the convention. But ordinary people who engage in extraordinary ventures are not average. Conklin certainly wasn't. She should be applauded not only for her effort, but for her eagerness to understand the issues and procedures of the convention. Conklin was not afraid to learn. If she needed something clarified, she was not embarrassed to ask questions. Nor was she afraid to voice her opinion, which she readily did. Conklin never let her voice be drowned out by Con-Con's lawyers, scholars or political heavyweights. Mr. Smith may have gone to Washington, but Conklin went to Con-Con.

Katherine

People still say that they want to "get Kay on the phone" to resolve some question regarding good government. She would have known the answer right off the top of her head.

—Betsy Cushman, *Kay Cushman & Con-Con & Me*

As she had done prior to Con-Con, Katherine Cushman spent her post Con-Con years working to improve government and protect the environment. The lifelong Dearborn resident studied reorganization of Wayne County government in the late 1960s as a member of the Committee of 99. As a member of the Dearborn Charter Commission, she helped rewrite the city charter in the late 1970s. Cushman also served two terms on the Dearborn City Planning Commission in the 1980s. In 1980, she served on the governor's Energy Awareness Advisory Council. Near the end of her life, Cushman chaired a committee to save the Rouge Woods and headed a group that fought successfully to stop Hines Drive from cutting through Ford Field.

When Cushman died unexpectedly from a heart attack on August 6, 1991, at age seventy-four, the *Detroit News* announced her passing as thus: "Katherine Cushman: Dearborn's Watchdog."[6] "Dearborn's Finest" continued to be recognized long after her passing.

Ann

One of the most respected among the women delegates is Miss Ann E. Donnelly, an attorney from Highland Park. She's representative of the younger force of females in the state who are holding down important jobs of their own in the communities in which they live.

—"Women Have Been Waiting,"
Saginaw News, November 12, 1961

Ann Donnelly continued to practice law after Con-Con ended. Donnelly was probably the female delegate that made the longest record at Con-Con. The convention's *Official Record* is evidence of Donnelly's professionalism and legal excellence. Donnelly was never intimidated by the brilliant legal minds or retired judges at Con-Con. One seasoned attorney who was being questioned by her during a convention floor debate responded, "I see that you are trying to trap me, Miss Donnelly. That's all right. I will be trapped."[7] The über-lawyer had her softer side. The psychology major enjoyed oil painting and sailing.[8] Donnelly died in 1984 at the age of fifty-nine.

Daisy

The Michigan Civil Rights Commission pays tribute to a woman who was one of the greatest civil rights leaders this state has ever produced.

—Michigan Civil Rights Commission Statement
on the Life and Contributions of Daisy Elliott

After six tries, Daisy Elliott was finally elected to the Michigan House of Representatives in November 1962. During her eighteen years as a state legislator, Elliott earned a reputation as an "unusual breed of politician" whose focus was always on serving the needs of her constituents and the people of Michigan. Elliott never let others, or her humble beginnings, define her. This was apparent in the way she dove head first into her work at Con-Con. If she was ever intimidated by the scores of attorneys, judges or university presidents, she never showed it. She was too busy learning, working and growing. She never forgot why she was at Con-Con or the people who sent her there.

Elliott is best known as the coauthor of the Elliott-Larsen Civil Rights Act of 1976. In 2020, Michigan governor Gretchen Whitmer renamed the Lewis Cass Building in downtown Lansing the Elliott-Larsen Building. It was the first state building named after a Black woman. Daisy Elliott died on December 22, 2015, at the age of ninety-eight.

Adelaide

Adelaide took on the responsibility of organizing the women in the state and often had to suffer the hardly concealed objections of the men. She called her group the Federation of Democratic Women.

—Helen Berthelot, *Win Some Lose Some:*
G. Mennen Williams and the New Democrats

Adelaide Hart spent the remainder of her life doing the two things she enjoyed most: teaching and working for the Democratic party. Hart's great capacity to learn, teach and take an interest in others remained throughout her life. When Tom Downs visited Hart several weeks before her death at age ninety-five, she was reading a book. Hart maintained contact with many old friends, as well as with their spouses and children. And she was still interested in making new friends. Several weeks before she passed, she was looking forward to meeting the son of an old friend who had planned to visit her in the nursing home.

Hart lived her life with an attitude of gratitude. She was grateful that she grew up in a house with loving parents and a devoted older sister. As Hart later said, "I've had a wonderful life, and I've enjoyed every minute."[9]

Lillian

*To trade unionists and UAW workers . . . the name of Lillian Hatcher
has a profound meaning.*

—"Hatcher Retirement Marks New Beginning,"
Michigan Chronicle, June 21, 1980

Sometimes a single decision can change the course of one's life. For Lillian Hatcher, that decision was going to work in the defense industry during World War II. Hatcher's meteoric rise from industrial worker to becoming the UAW's first Black female international representative is a story of hope and inspiration. When Hatcher hired in at the Chrysler Briggs-Connor plant on January 18, 1943, she was not looking for a career. She and her husband John had three children to support. John was subject to repeated layoffs as a Chrysler employee. He was lucky if he worked seven months out of the year.[10] Low wages paid to Black men often forced Black women to work. The couple needed money and defense work paid twice what Hatcher had earned as a hospital cafeteria worker. Thus, when Hatcher heard that Briggs Manufacturing was training women for defense work, she seized the opportunity and became one of the first seven Black women hired. At the time, Black women constituted only one thousand of the ninety-six thousand positions held by women in Detroit's defense industry.[11] Years later, Hatcher wrote, "To many families, the wife's earning meant the difference between bare subsistence and more adequate family support."[12]

Hatcher resumed her career with the UAW after Con-Con ended. Trade unionism was an important part of her life and marriage. The Hatchers entertained trade unionists from all over the world, inviting them to their home for dinner or to spend the night. Their deep interest in the labor movement was not only good for their marriage, but it kept them talking to each other.[13] The woman who simply wanted to give her children a better life spent a lifetime improving the lives of others. Lillian Hatcher died in 1998 at age eighty-three.

Dorothy

Dorothy Leonard Judd never held elective office, but it is no exaggeration
to say that she had as much influence on the quality of government and
public service in Michigan as any elected official.

—"Dorothy Leonard Judd," Greater
Grand Rapids Women's History Council

Dorothy Judd continued to work for good government and with the Michigan League of Women Voters after Con-Con ended. In December 1962, Judd was named as chairman of the Michigan Advisory Committee to the Civil Rights Commission.[14] In 1963, Governor Romney appointed her to the state Civil Service Commission where she served as chairwoman in 1965.[15] She resigned in 1969. Judd continued to fight for true county home rule years after Con-Con ended.[16]

With her long, rich family and civic history in Grand Rapids, Judd was referred to as the city's First Lady or First Lady of Politics.[17] She died in 1989 at the age of ninety. Like other family members, Judd was laid to rest in Fulton Street cemetery. She is the only family member included in a walking tour of the historic Grand Rapids graveyard.[18]

Ella

Many of us who have worked to build a strong two-party political
system in Michigan are deeply in Ella Koeze's debt for her countless
contributions over the years.

—George Romney, United Press International, "GOP Leader
Retires," *Traverse City Record-Eagle*, August 22, 1968

Ella Koeze continued to promote the Grand Old Party after Con-Con ended. She was active in Romney's 1962 gubernatorial campaign and the campaigns of Republican candidates for the state legislature. As a member of the GOP State Central Committee nomination committee in 1963, Koeze was tasked with helping to choose four Republican members for the bipartisan state legislative apportionment commission.[19] In 1964, Koeze was a delegate to the Republican National Convention in San Francisco. While at the convention, she was reelected to another four-year term as Michigan's National Committeewoman.[20] Koeze was named coordinator of the 1966 GOP campaigns for attorney general, secretary of state and State Supreme Court. The following year, acting Michigan governor William Milliken appointed Koeze to the Grand Valley State College board of control.[21] Koeze served on the board from 1967 to 1981.[22]

Koeze died in 1986 at age eighty. The Grand Valley State University Board of Control named one of its new student living centers on campus after her the following year.[23] Koeze's many years of service to the Republican party are well documented in the Grand Valley State University Special Collections and University Archives.[24]

Marjorie

> *My religion teaches me that I must make the very best of the short years I have in my control. I must not spend too much time and effort striving for temporal honors and distinctions.*
>
> —Marjorie McGowan, "A Chance to Help My Fellow Man," April 9, 1960

Marjorie McGowan never wavered from her infamous search and seizure position.[25] It followed her throughout her life.[26] Although it appears that McGowan never became a Republican, she had clearly burned her bridges with Democrats after Con-Con ended. Democrats were incensed when she campaigned for the proposed new constitution.[27] Columnist Judd Arnett wrote that he had been told that McGowan had been "forbidden" to return to Michigan to campaign for the new constitution.[28] When McGowan announced in early 1963 that she was leaving the Department of Justice to become one of Governor Romney's legal advisors, one Detroit newspaper headline read: "Dems Won't Miss Marge."[29] When Romney was appointed Secretary of Housing and Urban Development in 1969, he hired McGowan as a general counsel staff member.[30] McGowan returned to Detroit in 1977 to set up private practice. She passed away in 1980 at age fifty.[31]

McGowan was a de facto ambassador for gender and civil rights. She served as an example to women and minorities of what could be accomplished and perhaps inspired some of them to pursue their dreams.

Undoubtedly, she impacted lives as a Vista Maria school for troubled girls mentor, a Big Sister volunteer and as a pro bono attorney to the poor of Most Holy Trinity Parish in Detroit's Corktown.[32] McGowan spent the greater portion of her adult years as a lawyer doing volunteer work with many minority groups and the economically disadvantaged.[33] She utilized her credentials to reach audiences she may not normally have had access to. In her own way, Marjorie became her own civil rights movement.

Acknowledgments

Archivists are the unsung heroes of history. Historical writers would be lost without them. During the COVID-19 lockdowns, Michigan's archivists were a beacon of light in an otherwise dark and frightening world. In-person research was closed to the public and library and archival staff were working remotely from home. Staff went above and beyond the call of duty to assist me when I asked for help.

Michigan Tech archivists in Houghton researched the Ruth Butler collection for me. They scanned and emailed copies of articles, family letters and the Finlandia transcript of an oral history interview with Butler. At the time, I could find little information on Butler, and these documents helped immensely.

I can always count on the Archives of Michigan in Lansing for help whenever I visit or email questions. During COVID, they provided me with a Library of Michigan card so that I could access newspaper articles. They reactivated my card several years later when it came time to recheck citations during the final editing stage.

The Bentley Historical Library in Ann Arbor was also always quick to help with an online or in-person request. During COVID, they sent me the transcript of Lillian Hatcher's oral interview for the Trade Union Oral History Project, 1978–1979. It was illuminating. I was able to review the Katherine Cushman and Dorothy Judd collections in-person prior to COVID. During COVID, Bentley research staff found valuable articles on Anne Conklin and Ann Donnelly—the two female delegates that I found the least amount of information on. Livonia Public Library also emailed articles on Conklin that provided new information.

I really struck gold when I reached out to the Grand Rapids Public Library, Grand Rapids History and Special Collections Department. The Dorothy Leonard Judd papers they scanned and emailed were a historian's dream. The transcript of Judd's 1980 oral history interview was enlightening. The Greater Grand Rapids Women's History Council also deserves a big thank you for their guidance on researching Judd.

Copies of Ella Koeze's Con-Con journal were provided by the Special Collections and University Archives at Grand Valley State University. This filled a tremendous gap.

The Special Collections reference librarian at the St. Clair County Library System and the community engagement manager at Port Huron Museums scanned and emailed valuable articles on Vera Andrus.

Walter P. Reuther Library, Archives of Labor and Urban Affairs staff were also helpful.

My apologies if I have overlooked any archivists. I don't think I could have written this book without their help.

Special appreciation is extended to the Historical Society of Michigan for publishing my Con-Con 11 article and honoring me with a State History Award for the article the following year. They also asked me to give an online presentation about the women as part of their *History Hounds* lecture series. These opportunities generated interest in the book and respect for the subject matter. I cannot say enough good things about Michigan's oldest cultural organization and encourage readers to apply for membership.

Special thanks is given to Betsy Cushman, Con-Con 11 delegate Katherine Cushman's daughter. Despite my best efforts, I could not find a suitable group photo of the women. Betsy came to the rescue with a professional-looking photo from her mother's collection.

A tremendous debt of gratitude is given to Michigan State University Press director Elizabeth Demers for recognizing that the stories of the Con-Con 11 needed to be told. Although Elizabeth rejected the original biographical sketch format of the book, she suggested that I rewrite it as political narrative. I did, and the book is much better for it. Elizabeth has guided me along as she pushed my book through the peer review, acquisitions and publishing processes. MSU Press staff Judith Lakamper, Kristine Blakeslee, Anastasia Wraight, Nicole Utter, Megan Howarth, Jordan Ivonen, and freelance copyeditor Allison Janicki, were a pleasure to work with and very helpful. (My apologies if I have overlooked anyone.)

My sisters Pam and Valerie, brother David and his wife Myra—and childhood friends, Jacquie, Anna and Karen—deserve medals for listening about Con-Con and supporting my writing over the years.

My parents, Ralph and Delphine Liberato, deserve my deepest appreciation. Mom always listened patiently to *anything* I wrote. I could always count on her loving support and encouragement. Dad always believed in me too. He cared more about improving the lives of others than about building a political career. Perhaps that is why the Con-Con 11 resonated so deeply with me.

APPENDIX.

Senate Resolution No. 96

S enators Schuitmaker, Whitmer, Warren and Emmons offered the following resolution: A resolution to recognize and honor the eleven women who served as delegates to the 1961–1962 Michigan Constitutional Convention.

Whereas, One hundred forty-seven delegates gathered at Lansing to rewrite Michigan's Constitution; and

Whereas, Of the one hundred forty-seven delegates, only eleven were women; and

Whereas, The women were Vera Andrus, Ruth Gibson Butler, Anne M. Conklin, Katherine Moore Cushman, Marjorie Frances McGowan, Daisy Elizabeth Elliott, Adelaide Julia Hart, Lillian Hatcher, Dorothy Leonard Judd, Ella Demmink Koeze, and Ann Elizabeth Donnelly; and

Whereas, The women, five Democrats and six Republicans, were elected from districts across the state; and

Whereas, Identified in the official record by occupation, they included five homemakers, four teachers, two attorneys, one Realtor, and one union representative; and

Whereas, All had distinguished themselves with extensive participation in civic and political organizations and the leadership positions they attained within those groups; and

Whereas, Women were appointed to eleven of the fourteen convention committees, but as was typical of the times, none were appointed to chair a committee, and only three served as vice chairmen; and

Whereas, After the convention, several of the women delegates served in other political offices, such as the State Legislature and gubernatorial commissions, or received statewide recognition from notable organizations; and

Whereas, The success of the "Con-Con Eleven" encouraged more women to run for statewide public office, making women a greater and more powerful voice in the governance of our state; and

Whereas, The year 2013 marks the 50th anniversary of Michigan's current State Constitution, approved by voters in 1963; now, therefore, be it

Resolved by the Senate, That we offer this expression of our gratitude and admiration in honor and in memory to the eleven women of the 1961–1962 Michigan Constitutional Convention; and be it further

Resolved, That a copy of this resolution be transmitted to the only surviving member of the "Con-Con Eleven," Daisy Elizabeth Elliott, as evidence of our highest esteem.

(Adopted by Michigan Senate, October 17, 2013, https://www. legislature.mi.gov/documents/2013-2014/resolutionadopted/Senate/ htm/2013-SAR-0096.htm.)

Notes

INTRODUCTION

1. Pollock, *Making Michigan's New Constitution 1961–62* (George Wahr Publishing Company, 1962), p. 2.
2. Sturm, *Constitution Making in Michigan 1961–1962* (University of Michigan Institute of Public Administration, 1963), p. 20.
3. Sturm, *Constitution Making in Michigan 1961–1962*, p. 281.
4. *Con-Con: Triumph and Opportunity: Now to the Next Task*, Detroit News, Apr. 5, 1961, p. 12-B.
5. *Michigan Legal Milestones: 12. One Person—One Vote*, State Bar of Michigan, https://www.michbar.org/programs/milestone/milestones_OnePersonOneVote.
6. Sturm, *Constitution Making in Michigan 1961–1962*, pgs. 21, 23.
7. Sturm, *Constitution Making in Michigan 1961–1962*, pgs. 15–17.
8. Feingold, *Michigan Writes a New Constitution: Proceedings of the 1961 MCEP Faculty Workshop*, Michigan Center for Education in Politics, 1962, pgs. 15–16.
9. Pollock, *Making Michigan's New Constitution 1961–62*, p. 5.
10. Sturm, *Constitution Making in Michigan 1961–1962*, p. 17.
11. Pursuant to Article XVII, Section 4 of the 1908 Michigan Constitution, the

question of whether or not a constitutional convention should be called appears automatically on the ballot every sixteen years.

12. Pollock, *Making Michigan's New Constitution 1961–62*, p. 4; *CRC Special Report Michigan Constitutional Issues*, Citizens Research Council of Michigan, No. 360-02, Feb. 2010, https://crcmich.org/wp-content/uploads/rpt36002.pdf.

13. Feingold, *Michigan Writes a New Constitution*, p. 18.

14. *CRC Special Report.*

15. Sturm, *Constitution Making in Michigan 1961–1962*, pgs. 38–39.

I. OPENING DAY

1. *Con-Con Opening Festive Colorful Occasion . . .* , Lansing State Journal (USA TODAY NETWORK via Imagn Images), Oct. 3, 1961, p. 10.

2. Willah Weddon, *Daisy Elliott—Lady in the House*, Michigan Chronicle, Oct. 2, 1971, p. C1.

3. Daisy ran for Wayne County's 1st District in 1950, 11th District in 1954 and 4th District in 1956, 1958 and 1960. The Political Graveyard, https://politicalgraveyard.com/bio/elliott.html. *Candidate Honored by Sisters*, Michigan Chronicle (and Real Times Media), Jul. 31, 1954, p. 8; Candidate For House: *Daisy Elliott Wins Wide Endorsement*, Michigan Chronicle, Aug. 2, 1958, p. 3; *Seeking Election*, Michigan Chronicle, Jul. 30, 1960, p. A5.

4. Monica Scott, *Convention Firsts in 1961–62: Women, Black Delegates Included—Convention More Accessible Than Legislature*, Grand Rapid Press, Oct. 10, 2010, p. A13.

5. Elliott owned a beer and wine store. Michigan Chronicle, Aug. 29, 1959, p. 1. Elliott apparently also owned an apartment building at one time. *Daisy Elliott—Lady in the House.*

6. *Initiate League Chapter*, Michigan Chronicle, May 15, 1954, p. 17; Myrtle Gaskill, *Love Walked Right in and Stole M' Heart Away*, Michigan Chronicle, Dec. 5, 1953, p. 18.

7. *Daisy Elliott Wins Wide Endorsement.*

8. *Governor Whitmer Renames Downtown Lansing's Lewis Cass Building to the "Elliott-Larsen Building" to Honor Sponsors of Michigan's Landmark Civil Rights Law*, State of Michigan, Office of the Governor, June 30, 2020, https://www.michigan.gov/whitmer/news/press-releases/2020/06/30/

renames-downtown-lansings-lewis-cass-building-to-the-elliott-larsen-building.

9. *Con-Con Opening Festive Colorful Occasion . . .* , p. 10.

10. *Con-Con Delegates to Be Feted: Lansing Schedules Civic Celebration*, Detroit Free Press, Sept. 28, 1961, p. 3.

11. 1908 Michigan Constitution, Art XVII, Section 4 provided that the question of whether or not a constitutional convention should be called would appear automatically on the ballot every sixteen years.

12. Feingold, *Michigan Writes a New Constitution: Proceedings of the 1961 MCEP Faculty Workshop*, Michigan Center for Education in Politics, 1962, pgs. 15–19.

13. Allen, "An Interview with Retired Court of Appeals Judge Glenn S. Allen," interview by Tom Downs, Michigan Political History Society, Nov. 22, 1999, p. 7, https://jjblivinglibrary.com/allen-glenn-s/.

14. Bill McGraw, *Coleman Young: The 10 Greatest Myths*, Detroit Free Press, May 26, 2018, https://www.freep.com/story/opinion/2018/05/26/coleman-young-myths/638105002/.

15. Downs, "An Interview with Tom Downs: Attorney," interview by Bob LaBrant, Michigan Political History Society, Aug. 21, 1995, p. 42, https://jjblivinglibrary.com/downs-tom.

16. Hart, "An Interview with Adelaide Hart: Former Vice-Chair Michigan Democratic Party," interview by Tom Downs, Michigan Political History Society, Jun. 26, 1995, p. 34, https://jjblivinglibrary.com/hart-adelaide.

17. Jeffrey, "An Interview with Mildred Jeffrey: Community Activist," interview by Tom Downs, Michigan Political History Society, Dec. 28, 1995, p. 30, https://jjblivinglibrary.com/jeffrey-mildred.

18. Berthelot, *Win Some Lose Some: G. Mennen Williams and the New Democrats*, Wayne State University Press, 1965), pgs. 64, 93.

19. *Parties Being Very Polite So Far: Young Folk Enliven Sessions*, Saginaw News, Oct. 8, 1961, p. A-7.

20. *Bridal Shower Fetes Popular Miss Hatcher*, Michigan Chronicle, Mar. 18, 1961, p. B2; *Miss Hatcher Bride of James Williams, III*, Michigan Chronicle, Apr. 1, 1961, p. B2.

21. *At Convention: Masons Give Honor to Foreign Guests*, Michigan Chronicle, Apr. 28, 1962, p. B12.

22. *"Woman of the Year": Mrs. Lillian Hatcher to Receive Honor*, Michigan Chronicle, May 2, 1959, p. 5; *Mrs. A.A. Banks Speaker for Women's Council*, Michigan Chronicle, Nov. 28, 1959, p. A8.

23. UAW Women's Department: Lillian Hatcher Collection, Walter P. Reuther Library, Wayne State University, https://reuther.wayne.edu/files/LR000972.pdf.

24. Marie Teasley, *As Union Era Ends: Hatcher Retirement Marks New Beginning*, Michigan Chronicle, Jun. 21, 1980, p. 3.

25. Lillian Hatcher, *On the Labor Line*, Michigan Chronicle, Jun. 7, 1952, p. 20. When Briggs-Connor phased out, Local 742 became Local 212. Teasley, *As Union Era Ends*.

26. Elizabeth Hood, *Point of My Pen: Achievers: Models, Paper Missionaries?*, Michigan Chronicle, Jul. 5, 1980, p. 9.

27. *United States Commission on Civil Rights*, Detroit Hearings, Dec. 15, 1960, p. 351.

28. Mar. 17, 1960, Letter to Mayor Miriani by Detroit Housing Commission & Commission on Community Relations, Hearings before the United States Commission on Civil Rights, Detroit, Michigan, Dec. 14–15, 1960, p. 239, https://babel.hathitrust.org/cgi/pt?id=mdp.39015001791881&seq=7.

29. Judd, *A Delegate's Eye-View of the League of Women Voters and the Michigan Constitutional Convention*, Dorothy Leonard Judd papers, Collection 104, Box 1b, Folder 56, Grand Rapids Public Library, Grand Rapids History and Special Collections Department.

30. Vickki Dozier, *Porter Apartments, Once a Luxury Hotel, Part of Historical Society's Walking Tour*, Lansing State Journal, Jul. 26, 2018.

31. *A Lifetime in Grand Rapids, an Autobiography of Dorothy Leonard Judd, 1984*, Dorothy Leonard Judd papers, Collection 104, Box 17, Ch XI, p. 71, Grand Rapids Public Library, Grand Rapids History and Special Collections Department.

32. *A Lifetime in Grand Rapids, an Autobiography of Dorothy Leonard Judd, 1984*, Dorothy Leonard Judd papers, Collection 104, Box 17, Ch IV, p. 36, Grand Rapids Public Library, Grand Rapids History and Special Collections Department.

33. Donna Barnes, *Women Have Been Waiting: Now They're Having Say on Constitution*, Saginaw News, Nov. 12, 1961, p. A-7.

34. Jean Sharley, *3 Girls Get Together to Lay Down the Law*, Detroit Free Press, Mar. 3, 1956, p. 10.

35. Donnelly, *An Analysis of Proposed Article VI and the State Bar Pol*, 41 Mich. S.B.J. 41, 1962, p. 47.

36. *Edward Turner Reelected Head of NAACP Here*, Michigan Chronicle, Jan. 3, 1953, p. 1.

37. Bill Lane, *People, Places 'n' Situwayshuns*, Michigan Chronicle, May 28, 1960, p. C8.

38. *Two Charged with Brutality*, Michigan Chronicle, May 21, 1960, p. 4.

39. *Commencement—the End and the Beginning: U. of D., Wayne Will Graduate 2,700 Students*, Michigan Chronicle, Jun. 14, 1952, p. 23.

40. Issac Jones, *Shake-Up: Negro Aide "Shocked" by Firing*, Michigan Chronicle, Apr. 22, 1961, p. 1.

41. Issac Jones, *All Eyes on Marjorie McGowan; Lady Prosecutor "First" in Early Sessions Court*, Michigan Chronicle, Oct. 22, 1960, p. 2.

42. Interview by Paul Jalkanen with Ruth Butler, *Finnish Folklore and Social Change in the Great Lakes Mining Region Oral History Collection*, Finlandia Foundation National, Finnish American Historical Archive, Aug. 9, 1972, p. 16.

43. Ruth Butler family letter, Oct. 5, 1961, Ruth G. Butler Papers MS-420, Michigan Technological University Archives (Houghton, MI).

II. OCTOBER 1961

1. *A Constitutional Convention Report!*, League of Women Voters of Michigan, vol. 1, no. 1, Oct. 24, 1961; Dorothy Leonard Judd papers, Collection 104, Box 1a, Folder 18, Grand Rapids Public Library, Grand Rapids History and Special Collections Department.

2. Willah Weddon, *Daisy Elliott—Lady in the House*, Michigan Chronicle, Oct. 2, 1971, p. C1.

3. Downs, "An Interview with Tom Downs: Attorney," interview by Bob LaBrant, Michigan Political History Society, Aug. 21, 1995, p. 31, https://jjblivinglibrary.com/downs-tom/.

4. State of Michigan Constitutional Convention 1961 Official Record, p. 112, https://quod.lib.umich.edu/cgi/t/text/text-idx?c=genpub;idno=1749827 (hereafter cited as Official Record).

5. Bud Vestal, *It Works in Nebraska: Convention Is Much Like a Unicameral Legislature*, Saginaw News, Oct. 8, 1961, p. A-7.

6. Bud Vestal, *Labor Has Come of Age in Politics, Says Downs*, Saginaw News, Oct. 15, 1961, p. 7-A.

7. Official Record, pgs. 115–16.

8. Koeze, *Four Weeks of Con-Con: My Impressions*, Nov. 1, 1961, p. 4; Ella Koeze Weed papers, Grand Valley State University Special Collections and University Archives; Official Record, p. 118.

9. Sturm, *Constitution Making in Michigan 1961–1962* (University of Michigan

Institute of Public Administration, 1963), pgs. 78–79.

10. *Dorothy Judd's Personal Journal of the Michigan Constitutional Convention*, 1961, p. 3, Dorothy Leonard Judd papers, Collection 104, Box 1a, Folder 15, Grand Rapids Public Library, Grand Rapids History and Special Collections Department.

11. Official Record, pgs. 126, 127.

12. Official Record, p. 127.

13. Official Record, p. 167.

14. Delegate Proposal 1019; Official Record, p. 167.

15. Interview by Paul Jalkanen with Ruth Butler, *Finnish Folklore and Social Change in the Great Lakes Mining Region Oral History Collection*, Finlandia Foundation National, Finnish American Historical Archive, Aug. 9, 1972, pgs. 7, 11, 12, 13, 15.

16. *Proposals Hit Hopper: Con-Con Measure Seeks Election for Mining College Board*, Lansing State Journal, Oct. 12, 1961, p. 49.

17. Delegate Proposal 1021; Official Record, p. 170.

18. Delegate Proposal 1044; Official Record, p. 190.

19. Delegate Proposal 1100; Official Record, p. 214.

20. Delegate Proposal 1168; Official Record, p. 253.

21. Delegate Proposal 1676; Official Record, p. 382. Andrus and Nick Rajkovich cosponsored the proposal.

22. Delegate Proposal 1105; Official Record, p. 214.

23. Pollock, *Making Michigan's New Constitution 1961–62* (George Wahr Publishing Company, 1962), p. 45.

24. *Dorothy Judd's Personal Journal of the Michigan Constitutional Convention*, pgs. 8a, 8b.

25. Sturm, *Constitution Making in Michigan 1961–1962*, p. 172.

26. Official Record, p. 115.

27. Ruth Butler family letter, Oct. 5, 1961, Ruth G. Butler Papers MS-420, Michigan Technological University Archives (Houghton, MI).

28. Associated Press, *Says GOP's Fair Sex Cast Aside, Raps Party For Women's Roles*, Benton Harbor News Palladium, Oct. 11, 1961, p. 1; Liberato, *Con-Con's Petticoat Revolt: Women at the 1961 Constitutional Convention*, Chronicle magazine, Historical Society of Michigan, Summer 2023, pgs. 14–17.

29. Charles Harmon, *Plenty of Committee Posts: Convention War of Sexes Over, Women Agree*, Saginaw News, Dec. 31, 1961, p. 7-A.

30. *Vera Andrus, 80, Taken by Death*, Port Huron Times Herald, Sep. 1, 1976, p. 8C.

31. *In Constitution Hall: Plenty of Room for Visitors*, Lansing State Journal (USA

TODAY NETWORK via Imagn Images), Oct. 5, 1961, p. 45.

32. The Forum, Sept. 8, 1961. Cushman authored the first and second editions of *Dearborn 1951*, coauthored *Know Your Wayne County Government* and contributed to *Know Your State* (1968).

33. Cushman, *Dearborn and Its Government*, https://babel.hathitrust.org/cgi/ pt?id=mdp.39015071304482&view=1up&seq=1.

34. Official Record, pgs. 121, 131, 197, 411.

35. *Fearless Feminist: Battles for Women's Rights in Convention*, Lansing State Journal (USA TODAY NETWORK via Imagn Images), Oct. 10, 1961, p. 6.

36. Robert Popa, *This Con-Con Isn't Just a Man's Job*, Detroit News, Sep. 4, 1961, p. 1.

37. Official Record, p. 1002.

38. *Presidents of the League of Women Voters of Michigan*, League of Women Voters of Michigan, https://lwvmi.org/wp-content/uploads/2023/07/Past-Presidents.pdf.

39. *Dorothy Judd's Personal Journal of the Michigan Constitutional Convention*, p. 5.

40. *FountainFlow* magazine, in *A Lifetime in Grand Rapids, an Autobiography of Dorothy Leonard Judd, 1984*, Dorothy Leonard Judd papers, Collection 104, Box 17, Ch V, Grand Rapids Public Library, Grand Rapids History and Special Collections Department.

41. *Gets Reich Bid: Mrs. Siegel W. Judd Will Go to West Germany*, 1958, in *A Lifetime in Grand Rapids*, Box 17, Ch X.

42. *American Women to Visit Germany as Guests of German Government*, in *A Lifetime in Grand Rapids*, Box 17, Ch X.

43. *The New Germany—and German Women*, in *A Lifetime in Grand Rapids*, Box 17, Ch X.

44. Judd was an economics and political science major at Vassar and had taken courses in labor management. Dorothy Judd interview, Kent County Oral History collections, RHC-23, Grand Valley State University Special Collections, Sept. 17, 1971, p. 6.

45. Dorothy Judd interview.

46. Doug Bradford, *Katherine Cushman: Dearborn's Watchdog*, Detroit News, Aug. 9, 1991, p. 75.

47. Snow Woods Neighborhood Association, https://www.snowwoodsna.org/p/about-dr-edward-sparrow-snow.html; *The Snow Neighborhood*, p. 17, Dearborn Historical Museum, https://dearbornhistoricalmuseum.files.wordpress.com/2019/08/ dbntourguide20131-1.pdf.

48. Marguerite Austin, *Cushman, 1st LWV Historian*, Dearborn Press & Guide, Jun. 25, 1981.

49. *The Dearborn Historian*, Winter–Spring 1966, p. 8, Dearborn Historical Museum, https://dearbornhistoricalmuseum.files.wordpress.com/2015/03/vol-06-no-1-2.pdf.

50. President Stephen Nisbet, Official Record, p. 335.

51. Sturm, *Constitution Making in Michigan 1961–1962*, p. 73.

52. Official Record, pgs. 135, 163.

53. Official Record, p. 336.

54. Sturm, *Constitution Making in Michigan 1961–1962*, p. 57.

55. *Dorothy Judd's Personal Journal of the Michigan Constitutional Convention*, p. 7.

56. *Dorothy Judd's Personal Journal of the Michigan Constitutional Convention*, p. 5.

57. *Con-Con Notes: Civil Service Curb Sought by Brake*, Detroit News, Oct. 13, 1961, p. 13.

58. *Dorothy Judd's Personal Journal of the Michigan Constitutional Convention*, p. 9.

59. *Dorothy Judd's Personal Journal of the Michigan Constitutional Convention*, pgs. 9–10.

60. *Dorothy Judd's Personal Journal of the Michigan Constitutional Convention*, p. 13.

61. Dorothy Judd, Katherine Cushman, Elmer Radka, Burton Richard and William Ford were assigned to the subcommittee on natural resources. Local Government Committee Action Journal, Oct. 26, 1961, Bentley Historical Library, University of Michigan.

62. *A Lifetime in Grand Rapids*, Ch II.

63. *A Lifetime in Grand Rapids*, Ch XI.

64. The Dearborn Historian, vol. 6, nos. 1 & 2, Winter–Spring, 1966., https://thedhm.org/wp-content/uploads/2015/03/vol-06-no-1-2.pdf.

65. Education Committee Action Journal, Oct. 26, 1961, Bentley Historical Library, University of Michigan.

66. Charles Harmon, *Community Colleges Spotlighted*, Saginaw News, Oct. 29, 1961, p. 7-A.

67. Ruth Butler family letter, Oct. 5, 1961, Ruth G. Butler Papers, MS-420, Michigan Technological University Archives (Houghton, MI).

68. *Michigan Constitutional Convention Handbook 1961–1962*, https://babel.hathitrust.org/cgi/pt?id=mdp.39015071175932&seq=3.

69. Vickki Dozier, *From the Archives: The Hotel Olds*, Lansing State Journal (USA TODAY NETWORK via Imagn Images), Sept. 29, 2017, https://www.lansingstatejournal.com/story/life/2017/09/29/archives-hotel-olds/712009001/.

70. Vickki Dozier, *Porter Apartments, Once a Luxury Hotel, Part of Historical Society's Walking Tour*, Lansing State Journal (USA TODAY NETWORK via Imagn Images), Jul. 26, 2018. Porter Hotel is a stop on the Historical Society of Greater Lansing walking tour https://www.lansingstatejournal.com/story/news/2018/07/26/luxurious-porter-hotel-stop-historical-society-greater-lansing-walking-tour/834226002/.

71. *Dorothy Judd's Personal Journal of the Michigan Constitutional Convention*, pgs. 12–13.

72. *A Lifetime in Grand Rapids*, Box 17, Ch II.

73. Finance and Taxation Committee Action Journal, Oct. 25, 1961, Bentley Historical Library, University of Michigan.

74. Executive Branch Committee Action Journal, Oct. 25, 1961, Bentley Historical Library, University of Michigan. *Dorothy Judd's Personal Journal of the Michigan Constitutional Convention*, p. 12.

75. Official Record, p. 642; *Civil Service's Future*, Escanaba Daily Press, Feb. 4, 1963, p. 4.

76. Michigan governor George Romney appointed Judd to the Michigan Civil Service Commission in 1963. Judd chaired the Commission in 1965 and resigned in 1969. *Dorothy Judd: Civic Leader, Political Activist, Author*, Detroit News, Feb. 17, 1989, p. 12.

77. *Dorothy Judd's Personal Journal of the Michigan Constitutional Convention*, p. 11.

78. *Merit System Pioneer to Resign*, Detroit News, Mar. 23, 1969, p. 36. *An Evaluation of the Michigan Civil Service System: A Report*, Citizens Research Council, Report No. 288, Jul. 1988.

79. Albert H. and Emma M. Wheeler papers, 1938–1994, Bentley Historical Library, University of Michigan; Liberato, *Creation at Con-Con: The Birth of Michigan's Civil Rights Commission*, Michigan History magazine, Historical Society of Michigan, Sept/Oct 2024, pgs. 39–43.

III. NOVEMBER 1961

1. *First Lobbyists Register under Con-Con Rule*, Lansing State Journal (USA TODAY NETWORK via Imagn Images), Nov. 9, 1961, p. 14.

2. Judd, *A Delegate's Eye-View of the League of Women Voters and the Michigan Constitutional Convention*, Dorothy Leonard Judd papers, Collection 104, Box

1b, Folder 56, Grand Rapids Public Library, Grand Rapids History and Special Collections Department.

3. Joe Snyder, *Con-Con Report: Women in Politics to Stay*, St. Clair Shores Community News, Mar. 28, 1962, p. 16.

4. Feingold, *Michigan Writes a New Constitution: Proceedings of the 1961 MCEP Faculty Workshop*, Michigan Center for Education in Politics, 1962, pgs. 21, 30.

5. *9 Con-Con Plans Urged*, Detroit Free Press, Oct. 16, 1961, p. 3.

6. *Con-Con Notes: Wide Local Power Asked by League*, Detroit News, Nov. 21, 1961, p. 19.

7. *A Constitutional Convention Report!*, League of Women Voters of Michigan, Oct. 24,1961, p. 3.

8. *Complains of Lobbying*, Lansing State Journal, Apr. 19, 1962, p. 47.

9. State of Michigan Constitutional Convention 1961 Official Record, p. 283, https://quod.lib.umich.edu/cgi/t/text/text-idx?c=genpub;idno=1749827 (hereafter cited as Official Record).

10. Official Record, p. 277.

11. *Dorothy Judd's Personal Journal of the Michigan Constitutional Convention*, 1961, p. 16, Dorothy Leonard Judd papers, Collection 104, Box 1a, Folder 15, Grand Rapids Public Library, Grand Rapids History and Special Collections Department.

12. Sturm, *Constitution Making in Michigan 1961–1962* (University of Michigan Institute of Public Administration, 1963), p. 138.

13. Official Record, pgs. 300, 320.

14. Pat McCarthy, *Con-Con Votes to Quit March 31, Defers Action on Speeding Work*, Lansing State Journal (USA TODAY NETWORK via Imagn Images), Dec. 7, 1961, p. 8.

15. *Dorothy Judd's Personal Journal of the Michigan Constitutional Convention*, pgs. 14–15, 19.

16. *All About Women: Miss Andrus Guest Speaker*, Port Huron Times Herald, Nov. 20, 1961, p. 10; *Dorothy Judd's Personal Journal of the Michigan Constitutional Convention*, p. 21.

17. Pollock, *Making Michigan's New Constitution 1961–62* (George Wahr Publishing Company, 1962), p. 41.

18. Sturm, *Constitution Making in Michigan 1961–1962*, pgs. 111–12.

19. Official Record, pgs. 222, 285.

20. *Dorothy Judd's Personal Journal of the Michigan Constitutional Convention*,

1961, p. 20.

21. Official Record, pgs. 167, 191, 214.

22. Declaration of Rights, Suffrage and Elections Action Journal, No. 15, Nov. 16, 1961, Bentley Historical Library, University of Michigan.

23. Declaration of Rights, Suffrage and Elections Action Journal, No. 11, Nov. 18, 1961, Bentley Historical Library, University of Michigan.

24. Official Record, p. 319.

25. 1908 Michigan Constitution, Article II, Section 19.

26. Hart, "An Interview with Adelaide Hart: Former Vice-Chair Michigan Democratic Party," interview by Tom Downs, Jun. 26, 1995, Michigan Political History Society, pgs. 34–35, https://jjblivinglibrary.com/hart-adelaide/.

27. Education Committee Action Journal, Nov. 27, 1961, No. 12, Bentley Historical Library, University of Michigan.

28. Sturm, *Constitution Making in Michigan 1961–1962*, p. 87.

29. Robert Popa, *Draft Women for Guard, State Commander Urges*, Detroit News, Nov. 22, 1961, p. 3-A.

30. *Menominee "Lost" on State Map*, Lansing State Journal (USA TODAY NETWORK via Imagn Images), Nov. 19, 1961, p. 26.

31. Official Record, p. 271.

32. Williams got the nickname "Soapy" because his grandfather owned a toiletries business.

33. *Honor Williams*, Lansing State Journal, Nov. 14, 1961, p. 8.

34. *Old Friends*, Detroit Free Press, Nov. 15, 1961, p. 1.

35. Official Record, p. 265.

36. Local Government Committee Action Journal, Nov. 14, 1961, No. 13, Bentley Historical Library, University of Michigan.

37. *Dorothy Judd's Personal Journal of the Michigan Constitutional Convention*, p. 20.

38. *Dorothy Judd's Personal Journal of the Michigan Constitutional Convention*, p. 22.

39. Rockwell Gust Jr., John Shaffer and James Sterrett were also named to the subcommittee. Executive Branch Committee Action Journal, No. 14, Nov. 16, 1961.

40. Carl Rudow, *State Agencies Merged by Harmonious Con-Con*, Detroit News, Mar. 23, 1962, p. 8-B.

41. Con-Con would ultimately limit the number of departments to twenty. 1963 Michigan Constitution, Article V, Section 2.

42. Official Record, p. 269.

43. Official Record, p. 251.

44. Koeze, *Four Weeks of Con-Con: My Impressions*, Nov. 1, 1961, p. 9; Ella Koeze Weed papers, Grand Valley State University Special Collections and University Archives.

45. Local Government Committee Action Journal, Nov. 1, 1961.

46. Official Record, p. 263.

47. *Dorothy Judd's Personal Journal of the Michigan Constitutional Convention*, p. 16.

48. Sue Stark, *League of Women Voters Observing Anniversary*, Port Huron Times Herald, 1969.

49. Koeze, *Four Weeks of Con-Con: My Impressions*, p. 10; Ella Koeze Weed papers, Grand Valley State University Special Collections and University Archives.

50. Sturm, *Constitution Making in Michigan 1961–1962*, p. 146.

51. Official Record, p. 293.

52. *Dorothy Judd: Civic Leader, Political Activist, Author*, Detroit News, Feb. 17, 1989, p. 12.

53. *A Visit to Germany*, in *A Lifetime in Grand Rapids, an Autobiography of Dorothy Leonard Judd, 1984*, Dorothy Leonard Judd papers, Collection 104, Box 17, Ch X, Grand Rapids Pubic Library, Grand Rapids History and Special Collections Department.

54. Declaration of Rights, Suffrage and Elections Action Journal, No. 14, Nov. 15, 1961, Bentley Historical Library, University of Michigan.

55. Official Record, p. 296.

56. Resolution 47, Official Record, p. 320.

57. United Press International, *Con-Con Quits for Holiday: More Proposals Tossed in Hopper*, Port Huron Times Herald, Nov. 22, 1961, p. 1.

58. Official Record, p. 306.

59. Declaration of Rights, Suffrage and Elections Action Journal, No. 19, Nov. 30, 1961, Bentley Historical Library, University of Michigan.

60. Official Record, pgs. 331–32. Any delegate who wanted to present a proposal could still do so as long as she or he presented it to the drafting office by 5:00 p.m. on December 1. All proposals received by that date and time would be introduced at a subsequent date.

61. *Dorothy Judd's Personal Journal of the Michigan Constitutional Convention*, p. 21.

62. *Dorothy Judd's Personal Journal of the Michigan Constitutional Convention*, p. 11.

63. Official Record, pgs. 320–21.

IV. DECEMBER 1961

1. James Robinson, *Con-Con Passes a Deadline: 800 Proposals Swamp Staff*, Detroit Free Press (USA TODAY NETWORK via Imagn Images), Dec. 2, 1961, p. 3.

2. Ken McCormick, *All Work, No Play Makes Little Jack*, Detroit Free Press (USA TODAY NETWORK via Imagn Images), Dec. 10, 1961, p. 25.

3. Ray Courage, *Letter from Lansing: A Good Group*, Detroit Free Press (USA TODAY NETWORK via Imagn Images), Oct. 8, 1961, p. 33.

4. Carl Rudow, *Tough Con-Con Decisions Near as "Education" Sessions End*, Detroit News, Nov. 18, 1961.

5. *George Romney Is Target of Democrats*, Lansing State Journal, Dec. 5, 1961, p. 16.

6. Carl Rudow, *Harried Con Con Delegates Losing Nonpartisan Gloss*, Detroit News, Jan. 22, 1962, p. 8-A.

7. Pat McCarthy, *Con-Con Votes to Quit March 31; Defers Action on Speeding Work*, Lansing State Journal (USA TODAY NETWORK via Imagn Images), Dec. 7, 1961, p. 8; State of Michigan Constitutional Convention 1961 Official Record, pgs. 348, 353, https://quod.lib.umich.edu/cgi/t/text/text-idx?c=gen-pub;idno=1749827 (hereafter cited as Official Record).

8. Education Committee Action Journal, No. 16, Dec. 1, 1961, Bentley Historical Library, University of Michigan.

9. *Adelaide Hart Meets Democratic Leaders*, Sault Ste. Marie Evening News, Aug. 6, 1953, p. 2.

10. Interview by Paul Jalkanen with Ruth Butler, *Finnish Folklore and Social Change in the Great Lakes Mining Region Oral History Collection*, Finlandia Foundation National, Finnish American Historical Archive, Aug. 9, 1972, p. 7. When Northern Michigan University first opened its doors in 1899, it was named Northern State Normal School. "Northern's History," Northern Michigan University, https://nmu.edu/nmuhistory.

11. Hart, "An Interview With Adelaide Hart: Former Vice-Chair Michigan Democratic Party," interview by Tom Downs, Jun. 26, 1995, Michigan Political History Society, p. 11, https://jjblivinglibrary.com/hart-adelaide/.

12. Helen McLaughlin, *Interest in History Made Mrs. Ruth Butler, Houghton, Run for Michigan Con-Con*, Marquette Mining Journal, Dec. 4, 1961, p. 10.

13. Interview by Paul Jalkanen with Ruth Butler, p. 15.

14. Delegate Proposal 1635 sponsors included Judd, Cushman, Radka and Davis; Official Record, p. 364.

15. Official Record, pgs. 404, 406, 574.
16. Official Record, pgs. 405–6.
17. 1908 Michigan Constitution, Article VI, Section 8.
18. Official Record, p. 377.
19. Ken McCormick, *Ike Warms a Cold Day: Famed Charm Heartens Chilled Crowds*, Detroit Free Press, Dec. 14, 1961, p. 1.
20. *Dorothy Judd's Personal Journal of the Michigan Constitutional Convention*, 1961, p. 17, Dorothy Leonard Judd papers, Collection 104, Box 1a, Folder 15, Grand Rapids Public Library, Grand Rapids History and Special Collections Department.
21. Official Record, p. 335.
22. Delegate Proposal 1283. Cushman and Julius Sleder introduced Delegate Proposal 1282; Official Record, p. 298.
23. Delegate Proposals 1559, 1560, Official Record, p. 345.
24. Official Record, p. 362.
25. Official Record, p. 1140.
26. *Michigan Tech Asks New Name Plus Status*, Lansing State Journal (USA TODAY NETWORK via Imagn Images), Dec. 5, 1961, p. 7.
27. Delegate Proposal 1600; Official Record, p. 361.
28. Delegate Proposal 1206 was cosponsored by Follo, Perlich, Rajkovich and Spitler. Official Record, p. 273.
29. Delegate Proposal 1676 was introduced by Rajkovich and Vera Andrus. Official Record, p. 382.
30. Delegate Proposal 1533; Official Record, pgs. 342, 2480.
31. Pollock, *Making Michigan's New Constitution 1961–62* (George Wahr Publishing Company, 1962), pgs. 25, 32.
32. Koeze, *2nd Four Weeks of Constitutional Convention*, p. 4, Ella Koeze Weed papers, Grand Valley State University Special Collections and University Archives.
33. Pat McCarthy, *Con-Con Begins Home Stretch on Wednesday*, Lansing State Journal (USA TODAY NETWORK via Imagn Images), Jan. 2, 1962, p. 4.
34. Sturm, *Constitution Making in Michigan 1961–1962* (University of Michigan Institute of Public Administration, 1963), pgs. 78, 88.
35. Pollock, *Making Michigan's New Constitution 1961–62*, p. 32.
36. Official Record, p. 342.
37. Official Record, p. 346.
38. Charles J. Wartman, *The Spectator*, Michigan Chronicle, Dec. 16, 1961, p. 6.
39. Official Record, p. 414.

40. Lillian Hatcher Interview, *Trade Union Oral History Project, 1978–1979*, pgs. 46, 73, Bentley Historical Library, University of Michigan.

41. Marie Teasley, *As Union Era Ends: Hatcher Retirement Marks New Beginning*, Michigan Chronicle, Jun. 21, 1980, p. 3.

42. *With Babies and Banners: Story of the Women's Emergency Brigade (1979)*, https://www.youtube.com/watch?v=pa75V-tdBko.

43. *Dinner Event to Honor UAW'S Lillian Hatcher*, Detroit News, Jun. 15, 1980, p. 69.

44. *In Constitution Hall: Plenty of Room for Visitors*, Lansing State Journal (USA TODAY NETWORK via Imagn Images), Oct. 5, 1961, p. 45.

45. Official Record, p. 2634.

46. Sturm, *Constitution Making in Michigan 1961–1962*, p. 108.

V. JANUARY 1962

1. State of Michigan Constitutional Convention 1961Official Record, pgs. 464–65, https://quod.lib.umich.edu/cgi/t/text/text-idx?c=genpub;idno=1749827 (hereafter cited as Official Record).

2. 1908 Michigan Constitution, Article II, Section 10.

3. *Mapp v Ohio*, 367 U.S. 643 (1961).

4. Official Record, pgs. 511–12, 526.

5. Official Record, pgs. 2857–58.

6. Bill Lane, *People, Places 'n' Situwayshuns*, Michigan Chronicle, Jun. 9, 1962, p. C8.

7. *Shake-Up: Negro Aide "Shocked" by Firing*, Michigan Chronicle, Apr. 22, 1961, p. 1; *Forced to Pay into Slush Fund, Olsen Aides Charge*, Detroit Free Press (USA TODAY NETWORK via Imagn Images), May 18, 1961, p. 10.

8. *The Case of the "Missing" Prosecutor: When the Spotlight's Hot, Olsen Ducks It*, Detroit Free Press, May 18, 1961, p. 3.

9. United Press International, *Negro Romney Aide Opposed to "March,"* Detroit News, Jun. 21, 1963, p. 3.

10. United Press International, James S. Brooks, *Romney Aide Says She'll Pass Up "Freedom March,"* Battle Creek Enquirer, Jun. 21, 1963, p. 7.

11. Willard Baird, *Con-Con Retains Search, Seizure Provision*, Lansing State Journal (USA TODAY NETWORK via Imagn Images), Jan. 23, 1962, p. 14.

12. Official Record, p. 680.

13. Marjorie Eicher, *Detroiter's Boss Is Bobby*, Detroit Free Press, Dec. 26, 1962 (USA

TODAY NETWORK via Imagn Images), p. 6-C.

14. Official Record, pgs. 2858–59.

15. Official Record, pgs. 527, 531, 686–87; Willard Baird, *Con-Con Retains Search, Seizure Provision*, Lansing State Journal (USA TODAY NETWORK via Imagn Images), Jan. 23, 1962, p. 14.

16. Official Record, pgs. 521, 523, 526.

17. Official Record, pgs. 2885, 2887.

18. Declaration of Rights, Suffrage and Elections Action Journal, No. 33, Jan. 11, 1962, Bentley Historical Library, University of Michigan.

19. Official Record, p. 467.

20. 1963 Michigan Constitution, Article I, Section 9.

21. Emerging Problems Committee Action Journal, No. 4, Jan. 24, 1962.

22. Sheriff, prosecutor, clerk, treasurer and register of deeds, 1908 Michigan Constitution, Article VIII, Section 3.

23. Carl Rudow, *Reforms for Local Government Drafted by Con-Con Committee*, Detroit News, Jan. 14, 1962, p. 11.

24. Allan Blanchard, *1st Backers Offer Con-Con Goals*, Detroit News, Jan. 14, 1962, p. 11-A.

25. *Citizens Charge "Rubber Stamp" Con-Con Delegates Rapped*, Detroit Free Press, Jan. 22, 1962, p. 10.

26. Mrs. Lewis P. Tuttle, League of Women Voters Dearborn, *Women Voters Laud Delegate Cushman*, Detroit Free Press, Feb. 20, 1962, p. 4.

27. Associated Press, *CFM Director Hits at Both Parties*, Lansing State Journal, Jan. 28, 1962, p. 1.

28. Official Record, p. 615.

29. Official Record, p. 619.

30. Official Record, p. 618. Perras quoted from the statement that the superintendent of schools of Sault Ste. Marie had made at the education committee hearing in Marquette.

31. Official Record, p. 628.

32. Official Record, p. 636.

33. Declaration of Rights, Suffrage and Elections Action Journal, No. 36, Jan. 18, 1962, p. 3, Bentley Historical Library, University of Michigan.

34. Official Record, p. 643.

35. Official Record, p. 654–55.

36. Delegate Proposals 1522, 1523; Official Record, p. 342.

37. Delegate Proposal 1569 was introduced by Democrats Coleman Young, Daisy Elliott, Lillian Hatcher, Raymond Murphy, William Greene, William Marshall, Tom Downs, Adelaide Hart and Harold Norris on December 6, 1961; Official Record, p. 346.

38. Executive Branch Committee Action Journal No. 30, Jan. 4, 1962.

39. Executive Branch Committee Action Journal, No. 43, Jan. 31, 1962.

40. *"The Den Mother": Housewife-Politician Darling of Con-Con*, Detroit Free Press (USA TODAY NETWORK via Imagn Images), Jan. 28, 1962, p. 16.

41. *End Partisan Bickering, Romney Urges Con-Con*, Detroit News, Jan. 30, 1962, p. 13-A.

42. Frank Hand, *Claim Selfish Interests, Politics Hinder Con-Con: Mrs. Hart Says GOP Writes Platform*, Lansing State Journal (USA TODAY NETWORK via Imagn Images), Jan. 28, 1962, p. 1.

43. Official Record, p. 574.

VI. FEBRUARY 1962

1. State of Michigan Constitutional Convention 1961 Official Record, p. 1026, https://quod.lib.umich.edu/cgi/t/text/text-idx?c=genpub;idno=1749827 (hereafter cited as Official Record).

2. Carl Rudow, *GOP Reports Gains on Unity in Con-Con*, Detroit News, Feb. 24, 1962, p. 5-A.

3. Elizabeth Hood, *Point of My Pen: Achievers: Models, Paper Missionaries?*, Michigan Chronicle, Jul. 5, 1980, p. 9.

4. Lillian Hatcher Interview, *Trade Union Oral History Project, 1978–1979*, pgs. 15, 17, Bentley Historical Library, University of Michigan.

5. *Frank Hand, Claim Selfish Interests, Politics Hinder Con-Con*, Lansing State Journal (USA TODAY NETWORK via Imagn Images), Jan. 28, 1962, p. 1.

6. *To Neutralize Romney: Hare Would Delay Con-Con*, Battle Creek Enquirer (USA TODAY NETWORK via Imagn Images), Feb. 15, 1962, p. 24.

7. Committee on Executive Branch Action Journal, No. 14, Nov. 16, 1961.

8. Official Record, p. 739.

9. Official Record, p. 751.

10. Official Record, p. 1173; "SC4 Celebrates Official 100th Birthday June 11," SC4, Jun. 8, 2023, https://sc4.edu/news/sc4-celebrates-official-100th-birthday-june-11/.

11. Official Record, pgs. 1172–73, 2564.

12. Official Record, p. 1080.

13. Renamed the Coleman A. Young Municipal Center after the death of former Detroit mayor Coleman Young in 1997.

14. *Authorization for Interlocal Agreements and Intergovernmental Cooperation in Michigan*, Citizens Research Council of Michigan, Report 346, Apr. 2007, p. 7.

15. *Con-Con Notes: Wide Local Power Asked by League*, Detroit News, Nov. 21, 1961, p. 19.

16. Cushman and Julius Sleder offered Delegate Proposal 1282: *A proposal to authorize intergovernmental contracts*. Official Record, p. 298; Cushman and Glenn Allen introduced Delegate Proposal 1526: *A proposal to permit cooperation between the state, cities, counties, townships and other governmental subdivisions and to authorize persons holding office to serve on any governmental body established for cooperative undertakings*. Official Record, p. 342.

17. Official Record, p. 1134.

18. Delegate William Ford, Official Record, p. 1101.

19. Brown, *Then and Now: The Unaltered Drive of Dorothy Judd, Once High Priestess of Power*, Grand Rapids Press, Mar. 13, 1977; *A Lifetime in Grand Rapids, an Autobiography of Dorothy Leonard Judd, 1984*, Dorothy Leonard Judd papers, Collection 104, Box 17, Ch XIII, Grand Rapids Public Library, Grand Rapids History and Special Collections Department.

20. Bromage, *Constitutional Aspects of State-Local Relationships: Municipal and County Home Rule For Michigan*, Con-Con Research Paper No. 3, Citizens Research Council of Michigan, No. 203, Oct. 1961, p. 17.

21. Sturm, *Constitution Making in Michigan 1961–1962* (University of Michigan Institute of Public Administration, 1963), pgs. 215–16.

22. *Local Government Plans Debate before Con-Con*, Livingston County Daily Press and Argus, Jan. 31, 1962, p. 3.

23. James Robinson, *Home-Rule Issue Is Shelved: Con-Con Shifts Fight to Legislature*, Detroit Free Press (USA TODAY NETWORK via Imagn Images), Feb. 16, 1962, p. 3.

24. Robert Popa, *Foes Hit Home Rule Compromise Plan as "Lansing Rule,"* Detroit News, Jan. 31, 1962, p. 4-C.

25. Official Record, p. 1092.

26. Mrs. Lewis P. Tuttle, League of Women Voters Dearborn, *Women Voters Laud Delegate Cushman*, Detroit Free Press, Feb. 20, 1962, p. 4.

27. The Editorial Page: *Con-Con and Courage*, Detroit News, Jan. 28, 1962, p. 22-A.
28. Official Record, p. 1102.
29. Official Record, pgs. 1094–95, 1105.
30. Dorothy Judd, *Explains Position*, Lansing State Journal, Feb. 4, 1962, p. 10.
31. Official Record, p. 1350.
32. *Not Doing So Well: That's What They're Saying about Con-Con*, Saginaw News, Feb. 25, 1962, p. 7-A.
33. Official Record, p. 1325.

VII. MARCH 1962

1. *Con Con Delegate Adelaide Hart: Accuses Republicans of Refusal to Discuss Controversial Issues*, Michigan AFL-CIO News, Mar. 1, 1962, p. 3.
2. *Attendants Will Be Bright*, Saginaw News, Oct. 15, 1961, 7-A.
3. State of Michigan Constitutional Convention 1961 Official Record, pgs. 1698–99, https://quod.lib.umich.edu/cgi/t/text/text-idx?c=genpub;idno=1749827 (hereafter cited as Official Record).
4. Official Record, p. 1700.
5. Official Record, p. 1701.
6. League of Women Voters of Michigan Mar. 19, 1962, letter to delegates, Dorothy Leonard Judd papers, Collection 104, Box 1a, Folder 18, Grand Rapids Public Library, Grand Rapids History and Special Collections Department.
7. Official Record, pgs. 1613–14; Willard Baird, *Delegate Irked at Bridge Toll*, Lansing State Journal (USA TODAY NETWORK via Imagn Images), Mar. 18, 1962, p. 1.
8. Willard Baird, *Some Characters Enliven Con-Con*, Battle Creek Enquirer (USA TODAY NETWORK via Imagn Images), Mar. 18, 1962, p. 10; Virginia Baird, *Mrs. Butler Honored by State B and PW*, Lansing State Journal, May 10, 1962, p. 48.
9. Elaine Jennings, *Feminine Delegates, Con-Con Wives Find Much to Discuss*, Lansing State Journal (USA TODAY NETWORK via Imagn Images), Mar. 14, 1962, p. 33; Convention secretary Fred Chase announced during the daily announcements, "For those interested in football: the downtown coaches' club wishes to extend an invitation to the male members of the constitutional convention to attend the weekly Wednesday lunches at the Jack Tar Hotel . . . held throughout the football season"; Official Record, p. 255.
10. Official Record, p. 1404.

11. Official Record, p. 1867.

12. Official Record, p. 424.

13. Official Record, pgs. 1601, 1739–40, 377.

14. Official Record, pgs. 1743, 2778.

15. Official Record, p. 1325.

16. Robert Popa, *Con-Con's Snags Point to "Disaster,"* Detroit News, Mar. 29, 1962.

17. Donnelly offered Delegate Proposal 1168 on November 6, 1961. Official Record, p. 253; Williard Baird, *Would Forbid Graduated State Income Tax: Proposal Submitted by Martin,* Lansing State Journal (USA TODAY NETWORK via Imagn Images), Nov. 7, 1961, p. 10.

18. Tom Joyce, *Boost Given to Con-Con in Capital,* Detroit News, Mar. 15, 1963, p. 11-A.

19. 1963 Michigan Constitution, Article VI, Section 1; Official Record, p. 3384.

20. Official Record, p. 1495.

21. *Five Plans for State Judicial Reorganization Go to Con-Con,* Lansing State Journal, Nov. 23, 1961, p. 58.

22. Robert Popa, *5 Judicial Plans Given to Con-Con,* Detroit News, Nov. 21, 1961, p. 19.

23. 1963 Michigan Constitution, Article III, Section 8; Official Record, p. 1543.

24. Robert Pearson, *Con-Con Poses Threat to Recorder's Court: New Plan Would Kill Tribunal,* Detroit Free Press (USA TODAY NETWORK via Imagn Images), Jan. 29, 1962, p. 3. Detroit Recorder's Court was later abolished and merged with the third judicial circuit court. http://www.legislature.mi.gov/(S(yuy2bz45i05wl155g-clxjvqp))/documents/mcl/pdf/mcl-600-9931.pdf.

25. Official Record, pgs. 1380, 1402, 1405–6, 1409.

26. Tom Joyce, *Boost Given to Con-Con in Capital,* Detroit News, Mar. 15, 1963, p. 11-A.

27. Analyses of Con-Con's handling of the judicial article by Donnelly, Judicial Committee Chairman Robert Danhof and the Citizens Research Council of Michigan can be found in the following articles: Danhof, *Shaping the Judiciary: A Framer Traces the Constitutional Origins of Selecting Michigan's Supreme Court Justices,* Michigan Bar Journal, May 2001, pgs. 15–19; Donnelly, *An Analysis of Proposed Article VI and the State Bar Poll,* 41 Mich. S.B.J. 41, 1962, pgs. 41–47; *An Analysis of the Proposed Constitution,* Citizens Research Council of Michigan, No. 6, Dec. 28, 1962, https://crcmich.org/wp-content/uploads/apc06.pdf.

28. Official Record, pgs. 1921–22.

29. Official Record, p. 1905.

30. Official Record, p. 1922.

31. *Daisy Elliott—Lady in the House*, Michigan Chronicle, Oct. 2, 1971, p. C1.

32. Official Record, pgs. 1925–33.

33. Official Record, p. 1946.

34. Official Record, p. 1982; Liberato, *Creation at Con-Con: The Birth of Michigan's Civil Rights Commission*, Michigan History magazine, Historical Society of Michigan, Sept/Oct 2024, pgs. 39–43.

35. Official Record, p. 1994.

36. Official Record, p. 1999.

37. Official Record, pgs. 1946, 2000.

38. Official Record, pgs. 1946–49, 1999–2000, 2758–60.

39. Official Record, pgs. 2000, 2762.

40. Official Record, pgs. 2010–13.

41. Robert Popa, *Deadline Disaster Feared as Con-Con Crawls Along*, Detroit News, Mar. 29, 1962, p. 10-A; Robert Popa, *Con-Con's Snags Point to "Disaster,"* Detroit News, Mar. 29, 1962, p. 1.

VIII. APRIL 1962

1. State of Michigan Constitutional Convention 1961 Official Record, p. 2075, https://quod.lib.umich.edu/cgi/t/text/text-idx?c=genpub;idno=1749827 (hereafter cited as Official Record).

2. Official Record, p. 2143.

3. Official Record, p. 2145.

4. Official Record, p. 2187.

5. Official Record, pgs. 2188–89.

6. Official Record, p. 2199.

7. Official Record, pgs. 2211–12, 2746.

8. Official Record, pgs. 2758–63.

9. Official Record, p. 2272.

10. Official Record, pgs. 2279–80.

11. Official Record, pgs. 2278–87. The Michigan Supreme Court declared Rule 9 unconstitutional on February 6, 1963; Fine, *Expanding The Frontiers of Civil Rights: Michigan, 1948–1968* (Wayne State University Press 2017), p. 218.

12. *Gratiot FB Women Score Again!*, Michigan Farm News, vol. 42, no. 11, Nov. 1, 1964, p. 8.

13. Official Record, p. 2284.

14. Official Record, pgs. 2721–22.

15. Official Record, p. 2634.

16. James Robinson, *Road Cash Will Stay Earmarked*, Detroit Free Press (USA TODAY NETWORK via Imagn Images), Feb. 6, 1962, p. 12; William Baird, *Davis Plea Applauded, Rejected*, Lansing State Journal (USA TODAY NETWORK via Imagn Images), Feb. 6, 1962, p. 12.

17. Official Record, p. 2638.

18. Official Record, p. 828.

19. Emerging Problems Committee Action Journal, No. 13, Apr. 12, 1962, p. 4; Official Record, pgs. 2602–7; Mich Const 1963, art iv, § 52.

20. Official Record, p. 2439.

21. Official Record, p. 2489. The I Ain't Runnin' for Nothin' club was formed by delegate Claud Erickson to ease legislator fears that Con-Con delegates would challenge them in the next election; *Lack of Cooperation between Legislature and Con-Con Lamented*, Lansing State Journal, Apr. 15, 1962, p. 17.

22. Virginia Baird, *Mrs. Butler Honored by State B and PW*, Lansing State Journal (USA TODAY NETWORK via Imagn Images), May 10, 1962, p. 48; Official Record, pgs. 2622–27.

23. Pat McCarthy, *County Home Rule Section Approved without Changes*, Lansing State Journal (USA TODAY NETWORK via Imagn Images), Apr. 18, 1962, p. 10; 1963 Michigan Constitution, Article VII, Section 2.

24. Official Record, p. 2220.

25. Official Record, p. 2226.

26. Official Record, p. 2897.

27. Official Record, p. 2237.

28. Official Record, pgs. 2236, 2480.

29. Official Record, p. 2303.

30. Official Record, pgs. 2416–17.

31. Official Record, p. 2696.

32. Fine, *Expanding the Frontiers of Civil Rights: Michigan, 1948–1968* (Wayne State University Press 2017), p. 146.

33. Cobble, *The Other Women's Movement: Workplace Justice and Social Rights in Modern America* (Princeton University Press 2005), p. 73.

34. Dorothy Judd, Marjorie McGowan and William Hanna cosponsored the amendment; Official Record, p. 2888.

35. Official Record, pgs. 2888, 2912, 751.

36. Jeffrey, "An Interview with Mildred Jeffrey: Community Activist," interview by Tom Downs, Dec. 28, 1995, p. 42, https://jjblivinglibrary.com/jeffrey-mildred/.

37. Official Record, p. 2888.

38. Official Record, p. 2888.

39. Official Record, pgs. 2890–91.

40. Official Record, pgs. 2888–91.

41. Official Record, pgs. 2891–92, 2911, 2912.

42. Official Record, pgs. 2911–14.

43. Official Record, p. 2914.

44. Official Record, pgs. 2915–16.

45. Official Record, p. 2949.

IX. MAY 1962

1. Danhof, "An Interview with Judge Robert Danhoff," interview by Bob LaBrant, Michigan Political History Society, Sept. 21, 2001, p. 10, https://www.mipolitical-history.com/wp-content/uploads/2019/05/Danhoff-Bob_1.pdf.

2. State of Michigan Constitutional Convention 1961 Official Record, p. 1633, https://quod.lib.umich.edu/cgi/t/text/text-idx?c=genpub;idno=1749827 (hereafter cited as Official Record).

3. Pollock, *Making Michigan's New Constitution 1961–62* (George Wahr Publishing Company, 1962), p. 20; Sturm, *Constitution Making in Michigan 1961–1962* (University of Michigan Institute of Public Administration, 1963), p. 276.

4. Official Record, p. 1261.

5. Official Record, p. 1350 and p. 1404: Resolution 81:

> Whereas, It sometimes happens during the course of debate in committee of the whole, a substantial number of delegates are absent from the floor and do not attend the debate, but nevertheless are later summoned to the floor to vote without having heard the reasons offered on each side of the debate; and
>
> Whereas, Such votes are not based on the reasons set forth in the debate, and may in fact not be based on any reasons whatever; now therefore be it

> Resolved, That if any delegate shall leave the floor of the conven-
> tion during sitting of the committee of the whole, he shall thereafter be
> excluded from the floor until such time as a vote is taken on the issue
> then pending, except if he shall have been excused by the chairman
> before having left the floor.

6. Official Record, p. 2589.

7. Pat McCarthy, *Con-Con Delegates Study Change in Eminent Domain*, Lansing State Journal (USA TODAY NETWORK via Imagn Images), Dec. 6, 1961, p. 35.

8. Official Record, p. 2580; Sturm, *Constitution Making in Michigan 1961–1962*, p. 241.

9. Official Record, p. 3036.

10. Official Record, pgs. 2836–37, 3036.

11. 1963 Michigan Constitution, Article X, Section 2.

12. Official Record, p. 3043.

13. Cushman, *Dearborn and Its Government: A Comprehensive Handbook for the Citizen Interested in His Community Designed to Promote Active Participation in Local Government*, The League of Women Voters of Dearborn, 1952, https://babel.hathitrust.org/cgi/pt?id=mdp.39015071304482&view=1up&seq=1.

14. Official Record, pgs. 3088–90.

15. Official Record, p. 3090.

16. Official Record, p. 3092.

17. Official Record, p. 3092.

18. Official Record, p. 3092.

19. Dorothy Judd letter to Mrs. Marshall Barrymore, May 29, 1962, Dorothy Leonard Judd papers, Collection 104, Box 1b, Folder 56, Grand Rapids Public Library, Grand Rapids History and Special Collections Department.

20. Official Record, p. 2440.

21. Official Record, p. 3152.

22. Official Record, p. 3153.

23. Official Record, pgs. 3153–54.

24. Official Record, p. 3153.

25. Official Record, p. 3124.

26. Official Record, p. 3147.

27. Hart, "An Interview with Adelaide Hart: Former Vice-Chair Michigan Democratic Party," interview by Tom Downs, Michigan Political History Society, Jun. 26, 1995, p. 36.

28. *Education Plan OK'd*, Lansing State Journal (USA TODAY NETWORK via Imagn Images), May 9, 1962, p. 10.
29. Official Record, pgs. 3155–59.
30. Official Record, pgs. 3155–59, 3194.
31. Official Record, p. 3213.
32. Virginia Baird, *Mrs. Butler Honored by State B and PW*, Lansing State Journal, May 10, 1962, p. 48.
33. Official Record, p. 3214.
34. Official Record, p. 3239.
35. Official Record, pgs. 3254, 3265.
36. Official Record, pgs. 3265–68, 3270, 3273–74.
37. Official Record, pgs. 3272–75.
38. *Split-Off Discussed*, Lansing State Journal, Feb. 21, 1962, p. 12.
39. Coleman Young, *Each Outstanding in His Way: Negro Con-Con Delegates Make Unique Contribution*, Michigan Chronicle, May 12, 1962, p. 5.
40. Glenn Engle, *Democrat Is Hired by Romney*, Detroit News, Mar. 23, 1963, p. 1.

X. LAST DAY

1. State of Michigan Constitutional Convention 1961 Official Record, pgs. 3291, 3295, https://quod.lib.umich.edu/cgi/t/text/text-idx?c=genpub;idno=1749827 (hereafter cited as Official Record).
2. Official Record, p. 3156.
3. Official Record, pgs. 3300–3301, 3307, 3311.
4. Resolution 118, Official Record, pgs. 3312–16.

CONCLUSION

1. Associated Press, *Democrats Plan Drive against New Constitution*, Battle Creek Enquirer, Jan. 6, 1963, p. 25.
2. *The Constitution of the State of Michigan: Michigan's Constitutions*, https://www.legislature.mi.gov/documents/mcl/pdf/michiganconstitution1963asratified.pdf.
3. Pollock, *Making Michigan's New Constitution 1961–62* (George Wahr Publishing

Company, 1962) pgs. 45, 74; Sturm, *Constitution Making in Michigan 1961–1962* (University of Michigan Institute of Public Administration, 1963), p. 281.

4. 1963 Michigan Constitution, Article IV, Sections 2, 3, 4, 5 and 6.

5. McInerney, *A Brief History of Legislative Apportionment in Michigan*, Nov. 2, 1918, https://www.house.mi.gov/hfa/PDF/Alpha/Background_Brief_Apportionment_History.pdf. See also *Legislative Apportionment in Michigan*, Citizens Research Council of Michigan, No. 303, Dec. 1991, https://crcmich.org/wp-content/uploads/rpt303.pdf.

6. 1963 Michigan Constitution, Article IX, Sections 7, 14.

7. Pollock, *Making Michigan's New Constitution 1961–62*, p. 52.

AFTERWORD

1. Arthur St. Pierre letter to Vera Andrus, Nov. 7, 1962, St. Clair County Library, Special Collections.

2. *1st Woman Joins Houghton Council*, Detroit News, Apr. 14, 1966, p. 3-B.

3. Ruth Butler Exhibition Building—#3, https://www.upstatefair.net/wp-content/uploads/2019/07/Kiosk-Sign-Map-5.pdf.

4. Interview by Paul Jalkanen with Ruth Butler, *Finnish Folklore and Social Change in the Great Lakes Mining Region Oral History Collection*, Finlandia Foundation National, Finnish American Historical Archive, Aug. 9, 1972, p. 24.

5. *Ruth G. Butler, Active in Republican Party*, Detroit News, Mar. 31, 1981, p. 4-B.

6. *Katherine Cushman: Dearborn's Watchdog*, Detroit News, Aug. 9, 1991, p. 75; Eleanor Eaton, *Cushman, 74 Dies at Family Summer Home*, Dearborn Times Herald, Aug. 11, 1991; Daniel Lai, submitted by Anne Gautreau, *Dearborn Resident to Be Inducted into Michigan Women's Hall of Fame*, The Patch, Sept. 8, 2013.

7. State of Michigan Constitutional Convention 1961 Official Record, p. 2445, https://quod.lib.umich.edu/cgi/t/text/text-idx?c=genpub;idno=1749827 (hereafter cited as Official Record).

8. Donnelly graduated from the University of Michigan with a major in psychology. *Republican Women Varied Delegation*, Lansing State Journal, Nov. 12, 1961, pgs. 46, 51.

9. Hart, "An Interview with Adelaide Hart: Former Vice-Chair Michigan Democratic Party," interview by Tom Downs, Michigan Political History Society, p. 40, https://jjblivinglibrary.com/hart-adelaide.

10. Diane Haithman, *War Job Turned to Activist Career*, Detroit Free Press, May 3, 1984, p. 22.

11. Lewis-Colman, *Race Against Liberalism: Black Workers and the UAW in Detroit* (University of Illinois Press 2008) pgs. 17–18, 27.

12. Lillian Hatcher, *On the Labor Line*, Michigan Chronicle, Jun. 7, 1952, p. 20.

13. Lillian Hatcher Interview, *Trade Union Oral History Project, 1978–1979*, Bentley Historical Library, University of Michigan, p. 73.

14. United Press International, *Woman Heads Civil Rights Group*, Battle Creek Enquirer, Dec. 2, 1962, p. 12.

15. Doug Bradford, *Dorothy Judd: Civic Leader, Political Activist, Author*, Detroit News, Feb. 17, 1989, p. 2B.

16. *Then and Now: The Unaltered Drive of Dorothy Judd, Once High Priestess of Power*, Grand Rapids Press, Mar. 13, 1977; *A Lifetime in Grand Rapids, an Autobiography of Dorothy Leonard Judd, 1984*, Dorothy Leonard Judd papers, Collection 104, Box 17, Ch XIII, Grand Rapids Public Library, Grand Rapids History and Special Collections Department.

17. *Grands Rapid: Renaissance on the Grand—First Lady of Politics*, p. 140; *A Lifetime in Grand Rapids*, Ch XIII.

18. Garret Ellison, *Resting Place of Pioneers: Historian to Guide Fulton Street Cemetery Tours*, MLive/Grand Rapids Press, Sep. 3, 2014, https://www.mlive.com/news/grand-rapids/2014/09/fulton_street_cemetery_walk-th.html.

19. *GOP Sets Meeting on Apportionment*, Battle Creek Enquirer (USA TODAY NETWORK via Imagn Images), Apr. 12, 1963, p. 15.

20. *Michigan Caucus Is Saturday, Delegates Flying to Convention in Chartered Planes*, Battle Creek Enquirer (USA TODAY NETWORK via Imagn Images), Jul. 7, 1964, p. 7.

21. United Press International, *Milliken Names 3 to Grand Valley Board of Control*, Holland Evening Sentinel, Nov. 28, 1967, p. 26.

22. Grand Valley Forum, Vol. 005, No. 23, Mar. 9, 1981, https://scholarworks.gvsu.edu/cgi/viewcontent.cgi?article=1022&context=forum5.

23. Grand Valley Forum, Vol. 012, No. 05, Aug. 31, 1987, https://scholarworks.gvsu.edu/cgi/viewcontent.cgi?article=1004&context=forum12.

24. In January 1966, Koeze's husband of thirty-three years died unexpectedly of a heart attack. United Press International, *A.S. Koeze Dies at 68*, Holland Evening Sentinel, Jan. 20, 1966, p. 18. In 1973, she married Harold K. Weed.

25. Albert J. Dunmore, *Repeats Views on Search, Seizure: McGowan Maintains*

Position Despite Widespread Criticism, Michigan Chronicle, May 19, 1962, p. 1.

26. *Obituaries: Marjorie McGowan, Former Romney Aide*, Detroit News, Jul. 27, 1980, p. 7-B.

27. *Democrat Is Hired by Romney*, Detroit News, Mar. 23, 1963.

28. Judd Arnett, *States Caught in Noose*, Detroit Free Press (USA TODAY NETWORK via Imagn Images), Mar. 29, 1963, p. 52.

29. *Dems Won't Miss Marge: Ferency Calls New Job Definite Party Switch*, Michigan Chronicle, Mar. 30, 1963, p. 1.

30. Patricia Montemurri, *Marjorie McGowan, 48, Pioneer Black Attorney*, Detroit Free Press, Jul. 27, 1980, p. 78.

31. Although one newspaper obituary indicated that she was forty-eight at the time of her death, her Con-Con biography indicates that she was born in 1930.

32. *10th Annual Conference: Catholic Women to Meet Here, Luncheon Speaker*, Lansing State Journal, May 6, 1962, p. 56.

33. Official Record, p. 680.

Bibliography

ARCHIVAL COLLECTIONS

ARCHIVES OF MICHIGAN, LANSING, MI

Records of the Michigan Constitutional Convention, 1961–62.

BENTLEY HISTORICAL LIBRARY, UNIVERSITY OF MICHIGAN, ANN ARBOR, MI

Dorothy Leonard Judd Papers, 1935–71.

Katherine M. Cushman Papers, 1950–70.

Lillian Hatcher Interview, *Trade Union Oral History Project, 1978–1979*.

Other Publications (online).

Publications of the Convention (online).

FINNISH AMERICAN HERITAGE CENTER & HISTORICAL ARCHIVE, HANCOCK, MI

Interview by Paul Jalkanen with Ruth Butler, *Finnish Folklore and Social Change in the Great Lakes Mining Region Oral History Collection*, Finlandia Foundation National, Finnish American Historical Archive (Aug. 9, 1972).

GRAND RAPIDS HISTORY AND SPECIAL COLLECTIONS DEPARTMENT, GRAND RAPIDS PUBLIC LIBRARY, GRAND RAPIDS, MI

Dorothy Leonard Judd Papers, 1884–1985: Collection 104, Boxes 1a, 1b and 17.
  Soapes, Thomas. Oral History Interview of Dorothy L. Judd, Grand Rapids Oral History Collection, Box 1, Jan. 27, 1980.

GRAND VALLEY STATE UNIVERSITY SPECIAL COLLECTIONS & UNIVERSITY ARCHIVES, ALLENDALE, MI

Dorothy L. Judd interview, Kent County Oral History Collections, RHC-23, Sep. 17, 1971.
Ella Koeze Weed Papers.
Koeze, *Four Weeks of Con-Con: My Impressions*, Nov. 1, 1961.
Koeze, Jul. 28, 1962, speech. Personal collection.
Koeze, *2nd Four Weeks of Constitutional Convention.*

MICHIGAN TECHNOLOGICAL UNIVERSITY ARCHIVES, HOUGHTON, MI

Emily Riippa Schwiebert, *Flashback Friday: Inimitable, an Original,* Michigan Tech Archives Blog, Jun. 25, 2021, https://blogs.mtu.edu/archives/2021/06/25/flashback-friday-inimitable-an-original/.
Harold Bledsoe letter to Ruth Butler, Sep. 12, 1969.
Ruth Butler family letters, Oct. 5 and 16, 1961.
Ruth G. Butler Papers MS-420, Box 1, Folder 34–35.

ST. CLAIR COUNTY LIBRARY SYSTEM—SPECIAL COLLECTIONS, PORT HURON, MI

League of Women Voters of Port Huron articles.
Vera Andrus articles, letters.

HISTORICAL SOCIETY OF MICHIGAN, LANSING, MI

Liberato, *Con-Con's Petticoat Revolt: Women at the 1961 Constitutional Convention,* Chronicle magazine, Historical Society of Michigan, Summer 2023, pgs. 14–17.
Liberato, *Creation at Con-Con: The Birth of Michigan's Civil Rights Commission,* Michigan History magazine, Historical Society of Michigan, Sep/Oct 2024, pgs. 39–43.

MICHIGAN BAR JOURNAL, LANSING, MI

Liberato, Lynn. *Michigan Lawyers in History: Marjorie McGowan*, Michigan Bar Journal, Dec. 2020, pgs. 36–38, http://www.michbar.org/file/barjournal/article/documents/pdf4article4071.pdf.

MICHIGAN POLITICAL HISTORY SOCIETY, ORAL HISTORIES, LANSING, MI

Allen, Glenn. "An Interview with Retired Court of Appeals Judge Glenn S. Allen." Interview by Tom Downs, Nov. 22, 1999, https://jjblivinglibrary.com/allen-glenn-s/.

Danhof, Robert. "An Interview with Judge Robert Danhoff." Interview by Bob LaBrant, Sept. 21, 2001, https://jjblivinglibrary.com/danhoff-robert/.

Downs, Tom. "An Interview with Tom Downs: Attorney." Interview by Bob LaBrant, Aug. 21, 1995, https://jjblivinglibrary.com/downs-tom/.

Hart, Adelaide. "An Interview With Adelaide Hart: Former Vice-Chair Michigan Democratic Party." Interview by Tom Downs, Jun. 26, 1995, https://jjblivinglibrary.com/hart-adelaide/.

Jeffrey, Millie. "An Interview with Mildred Jeffrey: Community Activist." Interview by Tom Downs, Dec. 28, 1995, https://jjblivinglibrary.com/jeffrey-mildred/.

ARTICLES AND JOURNALS

Danhof, Robert. *Shaping the Judiciary: A Framer Traces the Constitutional Origins of Selecting Michigan's Supreme Court Justices.* Michigan Bar Journal (May 2001): 16.

Donnelly, Ann. *An Analysis of Proposed Article VI and the State Bar Poll.* 41 Mich. S.B.J. 41 (1962): 47

Feingold, Eugene. *Michigan Writes a New Constitution: Proceedings of the 1961 MCEP Faculty Workshop.* Michigan Center for Education in Politics (1962).

Kauper, Paul. *The State Constitution: Its Nature and Purpose.* Citizens Research Council of Michigan, Memorandum No. 202 (Oct. 1961), https://crcmich.org/wp-content/uploads/nature_and_purpose_of_state_constitution-1961.pdf.

BOOKS

Berthelot, Helen. *Win Some Lose Some: G. Mennen Williams and the New Democrats* (Wayne State University Press, 1965).

Cobble, Dorothy S. *The Other Women's Movement: Workplace Justice and Social Rights in Modern America* (Princeton University Press, 2005).

Collier-Thomas, Bettye, and Franklin, V. P. *My Soul Is a Witness: A Chronology of the Civil Rights Era, 1954–1965* (Henry Holt and Co., 2000).

Colman, David M. *Race against Liberalism: Black Workers and the UAW in Detroit* (University of Illinois Press, 2008).

Dillard, Angela D. *Faith in the City: Preaching Radical Social Change in Detroit* (University of Michigan Press, 2007).

Dunbar, William F., and May, George S. *Michigan: A History of the Wolverine State*, 3rd ed. (Eerdmans, 1995).

Fine, Sidney. *Expanding the Frontiers of Civil Rights: Michigan, 1948–1968* (Wayne State University Press, 2017).

Pollock, James. *Making Michigan's New Constitution 1961–62* (George Wahr Publishing Company, 1962). https://babel.hathitrust.org/cgi/pt?id=mdp.39015082040463&seq=5.

Sturm, Albert L. *Constitution Making in Michigan 1961–1962* (University of Michigan Institute of Public Administration, 1963). https://babel.hathitrust.org/cgi/pt?id=mdp.39015028398819&view=1up&seq=234&skin=2021.

ONLINE RESOURCES

Citizens Research Council of Michigan, "An Analysis of the Proposed Constitution," Dec. 1962, https://crcmich.org/publications/an-analysis-of-the-proposed-constitution.

Citizens Research Council of Michigan, "A Brief Michigan Constitutional History," No. 360–02, Feb. 2010, https://crcmich.org/wp-content/uploads/rpt36002.pdf.

Citizens Research Council of Michigan Special Report, "General Revision of the Michigan Constitution," No. 360–01, Feb. 2010, http://crcmich.org/PUBLICAT/2010s/2010/rpt360.pdf.

Conyers, John Jr. "Tribute to the Trade Union Leadership Council, Vol. 141, No. 190, Nov. 30, 1995, Congressional Record, https://www.govinfo.gov/content/pkg/

CREC-1995–11–30/html/CREC-1995–11–30-pt1-PgE2276.htm.

Cushman, Katherine. *Dearborn and Its Government: A Comprehensive Handbook for the Citizen Interested in His Community Designed to Promote Active Participation in Local Government.* The League of Women Voters of Dearborn, 1952. https://babel.hathitrust.org/cgi/pt?id=mdp.39015071304482&view=1up&seq=1.

Hearings before the United States Commission on Civil Rights, Detroit, Michigan, Dec. 14–15, 1960, https://babel.hathitrust.org/cgi/pt?id=mdp.39015001791881&seq=7.

Michigan Civil Rights Commission, "Statement on the Life and Contributions of Daisy Elliott," Jan. 25, 2016, https://www.michigan.gov/documents/mdcr/Elliott_resolution_color_511973_7.pdf.

"Michigan Constitutional Convention Handbook 1961–1962," https://babel.hathitrust.org/cgi/pt?id=mdp.39015071175932&seq=3.

National Municipal League, "Model State Constitution Sixth Edition," 1963, https://babel.hathitrust.org/cgi/pt?id=mdp.39015033711493&seq=1.

1908 Michigan Constitution, https://babel.hathitrust.org/cgi/pt?id=mdp.39015071175460&seq=9.

1963 Michigan Constitution, https://www.legislature.mi.gov/Laws/MCL?objectName=mcl-Constitution.

State Bar of Michigan, "Michigan Legal Milestones: 12. One Person—One Vote," https://www.michbar.org/programs/milestone/milestones_OnePersonOneVote.

State of Michigan Constitutional Convention 1961 Official Record. https://quod.lib.umich.edu/cgi/t/text/text-idx?c=genpub;idno=1749827.

VIDEOS

Michigan Can Lead the Way: The Story of a Constitutional Convention, https://vimeo.com/2563977.

With Babies and Banners: Story of the Women's Emergency Brigade (1979), https://www.youtube.com/watch?v=pa75V-tdBko.

Index